Kalki Purana

The Puranas are the best fusion of Indian ethos and literature. They contain the triumphs and tribulations of mankind. The eighteen Puranas relate the tales of duty and action, sins and virtues through the life and events of divine icons.

'Kalki Purana', despite being one of the 'Upapuranas', has its own significance. Although, according to 'Mahabharat', Kalki incarnation is yet to take place, the narration describes his actions in the past tense, and it has borrowed heavily from Vishnu Purana and Srimad Bhagawata Purana. At times the description of the story of Lord Kalki's marriage with the princess of Srihala Dweep, Padma, throws the images also conjured up in the Medieval Hindi epic 'Padamavata' by Malik Mohammad Jayasi. May be the latter was influenced by this Purana. But that clearly reveals that this 'Kalki Upapurana' did exist in and around 14th century A.D. when Jayasi wrote his above-mentioned magnum opus.

Kalki Purana

B.K. Chaturvedi

DIAMOND BOOKS

© Publisher

Publisher	:	**Diamond Pocket Books (P) Ltd.**
		X-30, Okhla Industrial Area, Phase-II
		New Delhi-110020
Phone	:	011-40712200
E-mail	:	sales@dpb.in
Website	:	www.dpb.in

Kalki Puran
By : B. K. Chaturvedi

Contents

Preface

Puranas literally mean something ancient and particularly they refer to the ancient records. In fact in the absence of the tradition of keeping historical records in a chronological order in ancient India, these Puranas emerge as important documents. They, in an allegorical manner, reveal the basic values that have been ingrained in a particular race or faith, apart from other social Indian details of the eras gone by. In every cycle of time, the Hindu Scriptures claim, there occurs a Vedavyas who edits, vets, compiles and even writes these Puranas with unbiased objectivity. Every one is not entitled to do this job. Vedavyas is supposed to be the most learned, experienced and enlightened person of the Age. As the name suggests the term 'Vedavyas' itself means someone who is like a diameter if the entire knowledge i.e. Vedas are likened to a circle. This actually means the most learned person of the age. It could be more than one. In fact all the Puranas, the Mahabharata, Srimad Bhagwata etc. that are supposed to have been written by one Vedavyas may have been written or compiled by many Vedavyases and perhaps the last one, Krishna Dweipayana, may have been the last one to edit them. As the historical records claim apart from what Vedvyas (Krishna Dweipayana) might have done, the last time it was duly edited and compiled was in the 5th-6th A.D. under the Gupta Reign which is said to be the golden-age of the Indian history. It was perhaps then that the need was felt to write this Purana, called Kalki Purana. Hence the doubt about its authenticity as it is not listed in the standard eighteen Puranas, simply because it was not written by that Vedavyas as it was composed much later. Nevertheless it also reveals the determination of the faith to strengthen its psychological composure at a period when attacks from the alien forces had restarted, almost a millennium after Alexander's invasion. Moreover, as the text itself suggests it must have been written when the Buddhist rulers were in power and the 'Mlechcha' invasions had started taking place. Hence the repeated reference of the two groups of the people described as adversary.

Nevertheless, Kalki Purana, though it is one of the Upapuranas has its own importance. Although according to the Mahabharat, incarnation of Kalki is yet to take place, this Upapurana describes his doing in the past tense. Also, by certain description of Lord Kalki, it is apparent that it has borrowed heavily from Vishnu-Purana and the Srimad Bhagwata Purana. At times the description of the story of Lord Kalki's marriage with the princess of Srihala Dweep, Padma, throws the images also conjured up in the Medieval Hindi epic 'Padamavata' by Malik Mohammad Jayasi. May be the latter was influenced by this Purana. But that clearly reveals that this 'Kalki Upapurana' did exist in and around 14th century A.D. when Jayasi wrote his above-mentioned magnum opus.

It has been the endeavour to keep the narration interesting. Hence some of the prayers, ovations or hymns have been included in the essence-translation form.

Lastly, the compiler is very grateful to Sri Narendra Kumar of Diamond Pocket Books for allowing him to do this work freely and rationally.

B.K. Chaturvedi

1
Prelude And Early Life Of Lord Kalki

Long ago Sootaji (an authority on the narration of the mythological tales and stories), engaged in deep worship of Lord Vishnu, Lord Supreme, adorable by all the deities and seers, said in feelingful voice: "O Lord! I reverence thee with all my heart and mind. You are called Nara-Narayan, whose mere frown is enough to incinerate all the iniquitous tyrants and reveal the reality through his own illusive creation – the Maya; whose benign glance is just enough to grant the worshipper the best nook in all the top realms. You appear on the earth in a variety of forms to set right the order of propriety. May you incarnate yourself again in the form of Kalki to ensure welfare of every being of this world."

When Shaunak and other holy sages saw Sootaji so deeply involved in the worship of Lord Hari in the holy region of Nemisharanya, they asked him: "O best of the seers! You are well aware of all the just nuances of the Dharma, a great scholar and omniscient by the grace of Lord Hari. Please tell us in detail as to what would cause Lord Vishnu to appear in the form of Kalki incarnation. Who is this Kalki? Where would he be born and how would he triumph over the disturbances then agitating the earth? How would he come to rule over the entire earth? What sort of penances and strict disciplines that one should observe to get to that envisaged status? What would be those factors that would cause the decay in the moral values and give rise to the downright immoral traits? Please satisfy our ardent curiosity and describe in detail about Kalki incarnation of Lord Vishnu."

Hearing this query from the holy sages and realising their ardent curiosity for learning about the Kalki incarnation, Soota first concentrated his mind on Lord Hari and getting enthralled by this remembrance and the Lord's grace he thus addressed the sages: "O high sages! Listen! I tell you in detail about Kalki incarnation. Very long ago once the Veena-player, Naradji, had asked Brahmaji about this wondrous story. Whatever Narad heard about it from Brahma was communicated by him to my exalted guru (mentor) Shree Vedavyasji. Vedavyasji told about it to his very precocious child Brahmaratra (Shukadeva) who narrated it to Abhimanyu's son Vishnuraata (Parikshit) at the conclusion of the great battle of Mahabharat. The holy discourse continued for about a week. The narrator and the listener both obtained salvation by the grace of the holy tale. This story was again retold by Sage Markandeya and Shukadeva when other high sages expressed their curiosity to learn about it. This holy tale, which is about to happen in future, was abridged by Shukadeva for its easier comprehension. Now detecting your unflinching faith and ardent curiosity I recite it again to you. Since you all are most deserving listeners, you must hear it with rapt attention." (Then Sootaji narrated this story).

When Lord Krishna, deeming the end of the Dwapar to be nigh and all his duties completed felt relieved, he left for the sea-shore where, according to the divine scheme, he was hit by a fowler's arrow in the sole of his feet. Kalki Avataar (Incarnation) was supposed to have taken place after Lord Krishna (Vishnu's) return to his Exalted Realm, Vaikuntha. Now listen to the main story:

"When the period of Pralaya was over and Brahma thought of starting the process of creation, he created a deadly dark affliction from his back. This affliction is called Maleen Pataka[1] (a very dark and deadly sinful object). When that Pataka grew up it came to be known Adharma (impropriety). Those who learn fully about this Adharma's lineage and progeny stay away from sin. The name of Adharma's wife was Mithya (falsehood). She had cat-like fickle eyes, and was extremly attractive and comely. Their union brought forth a son of very fiery temperament. Adharma called him Dambha (Vanity). This union also had a daughter called Maya (illusion), capable of easily drawing

---

1.   In fact this narration liberally uses allegory to convey the growth of Kaliyuga and its obnoxious offshoots. Hence it should be taken in the same light.

beings toward sin. Maya passed a lot of time with Dambha to get a son called Lobha (greed) and a daughter called Nikriti (dishonesty). When grown up Lobha and Nikriti also established sexual relations to breed a very indomitable son called Krodha (anger), and a daughter called Himsa (violence). As the names suggest, both of them were totally devoid of any noble feelings. It was the union of Krodha and Himsa that bred the world-destroying being called Kali (Kaliyuga)"

"Right at the time of his birth Kali carried an Upaasthi (a small bone) and his entire body complexion was sooty and dark. This huge-being, with a terrible tongue and an obnoxious smell about his entire physique, chose gambling, liquor, woman and gold as his permanent abodes. Meanwhile, Krodh and Himsa also produced a horrible daughter who was as horrendous as Kali had been. She established union with Kali to produce deadly son called Bhayanak and a daughter called Mrityu (death). Bhayanaka established union with Mrityu to produce a son called Niraya and a daughter called Yatana (torture) This way Maleen Pataka, produced by Brahma's back, had a horrible lineage which produced illimitable progeny. All of their descendants were highly immoral, iniquitious, encourager of the vile tendencies, indifferent or hostile to the gods and a positive nuisance to all those intending to tread the righteous path. They created such a havoc in the world that people began to yell for getting succour from the divine powers."

"These followers of King Kali had assumed human forms. They created animal-like lust in the population as much as to reduce into smithereens all the norms of propriety and noble deeds. With the result, the whole world was filled with iniquitous and cantankerous people. They made the Brahmanas eschew their noble path, the Kshatriyas behave like decoits, the Vaishyas (traders) as thieves and the Shoodras as the veritable scum of the society. The disciples began to defy their mentors, the sons became hostile to their fathers and elders, young men and women began to marry for the sake of slaking their carnal lust, friends became enemies and the scholars turned into hypocrites. The upholders of the law or order felt entirely incompetent to check the chaos setting in.

"The earth's productivity started to wane, the rivers changed their course and all the norms of society were thrown to winds. The nobles were subjected to great tortures and so they had to get to the inaccessible and deserted mountains; they had to survive eating fruits, foliage and raw meat. Even in this first stage of Kaliyuga the people had started condemning the holy incarnations including Lord Krisha, thus far the last incarnation of Lord Vishnu.

"By the time the second phase of Kaliyuga began, the conditions became so horrible that people forgot the name of God. Chaos reigned everywhere. By the third phase all progeny of the people were devoid of their clans and lineage as most of them were Varna-sankar (cross-breed). There remained no distinction of a class or category. All noble deeds and traditions remained confined to books only. Thus till the advent of the fourth phase of Kaliyuga, all the noble endeavours like seeking education, performing the Veda-ordained Yagya, god-worship, name-chanting, rituals etc. vanished from the surface of the earth. When the deities failed to receive their nourishment through the Yagya offerings, a group of them went to Brahma yelling for succour. They had the earth also accompanying them in the form of a cow. The conditions in the Brahma's realm were ideal. The sages were chanting the holy mantras and Yagya smoke was keeping the directions sweetly perfumed. Brahma welcomed the divine delegation and asked them to take their seats. Listening to their complaints sympathetically, Brahma, the Creator, said: "I am not as competent to provide you the succour. Only Lord Hari (Vishnu) could provide you the succour to put again the rule of propriety on the even keel." Then taking all of them along, he reached the grand realm of Lord Hari (Vishnu), Vaikuntha.

Lord Vishnu heard them patiently and said: "Surely I'd provide you the succour." Then explaining as to how he would do so, he gave the details of his mode of working. Dilating on the divine scheme to provide the earth and the deities their much needed succour, Brahma explained that Lord Hari would incarnate Himself in the house of his devotee called Vishnu Yasha, in the village called Sambhala. His mother's name, the wife of Vishnu Yasha, would be Sumati. All the gods would also incarnate themselves at the proper position including Lord Hari's eternal spouse Lakshmi. She would get birth as the daughter of the Sinhala Dweepa's King, from Raja Vrihadvatha's queen Kaumudi's womb. Then Lakshmi's name would be Padma. "Lord Hari will also deputise two earthly kings called Manu and Devapi who will help Him in the mission. Since this arrangement is perfect and entirely satisfactory to you all, you all should now return to your realms. But you must all be ready to incarnate on the earth at my inkling. Since things cannot be held under control from this far-off Milk-Ocean, we must go to the earth to set the rule of law, order and proprieity after eliminating the rogues. This is the only foolproof and time tested method of providing succour to earth and re-establish the divine order." Then reassuring the Earth in a cow's form, Vishnu said: "Go back to your place. Now leave your worries to me as I shall soon remove them." Continuing the narration, Sootaji told the assembly of the high sages that thus repeatedly assured by Lord Hari that Satya Yuga like conditions shall be re-established on the earth, the earth and the divinities felt relief.

And in accordance with the assurance that Lord Hari had given to the divinities, He began to fulfil his commitment. In due time, he entered the womb of Sumati – the wife of Vishnu Yasha. As he did so, the earth and its entire beings felt a surging wave of happiness passing through their consciousness. The birds and beasts, man and woman, the rivers and oceans felt supremely delighted. The manes and the deities who get nourishment from the Yagya offerings also became optimistic in the hope of regaining their health and vitality. The Gandharvas, Kinnars and the Apsaras (divine danseuses) began to sing in glee at the prospect of seeing the incarnation of the Supreme Spirit. The whole atmosphere was changed with a supreme delight. It was on the bright fortnight of the lunar mouth of Vaishakha, on the 12th lunar tithi, that Lord Vishnu took birth as Kalki in Vishnu Yasha's house. The parents were besides themselves with joy and gratitude, finding Lord Almighty taking birth as their son. It was indeed a matter of great pride to have such a son in their house. At that moment the gods assembled in the sky to sing paens of Lord Hari in ecstatic delight.

When Lord was born as Kalki incarnation, Mother Ambika came forth to hack off the placenta. River Ganga came there with her holy water to wash off the impieties of the womb covering the child. The whole scene reminded the spectacle of Lord Krishna's birth in Gokula. The 'Matrikas' sang the gratulatory songs. Having learnt about the holy birth Brahma asked the Vaayu Dev (Wind-god) to repair to the village Sambhal and request the Lord: "O Lord! Your four armed form is rarely seen even by the high deities. Hence, Lord, you must leave this form and appear in a normal human child's form. Else, these ignorant beings of the earth would publicise about your birth to set in motion the evil forces to cause hurdles in your way." Vaayudev immediately repaired to Sambhal and conveyed the message. Lord Hari quickly withdrew his four-armed form and appeared as a normal human infant. The parents, seeing the change of their son's form, were rather bewildered. But deeming themselves to have been bewildered in their own affection-filled infatuation, they realised that their son was actually a two-armed infant. As the birth had taken place the sinners felt uncontrollably pulverised with an unknown fear. People began to assemble at Vishnu Yasha's house who gratefully donated a hundred cows adorned with golden onrmaments to Brahmanas. Then the delighted father invited the Veda-reading Brahmanas and high sages to come to his place for giving his son a fair name. But the message spread far and wide that in the house of Vishnu Yasha, Lord Supreme had appeared as the son. In order to have the Holy Darshana, Lord Parashuram, Kripacharya, Vedavyas, Ashwatthama and other high personages[1] came to the house of Vishnu Yasha.

Deeming all the guests as brilliant as the sun, Vishnu Yasha honoured them reverentially and established them on the high seats. They were blessed with the Holy Darshana of the divine child sitting smugly on his father's lap. It was the sportive play of the Divine Lord which brought him to incarnate there. He was adored and saluted by all the high personages. Since He was incarnate for the sake of ridding the earth of the rogues and strengthen the noble values in the Kali Age, the boy was given 'Kalki' name.

"When the ceremonies were over and the high personages returned to their abodes, Kalki Maharaj began

---

1.   Mythologically all these personages are immortal.

to grow in his mortal parents' house the same way as the Moon grows in the bright half," said Sootaji, adding: "He was reared with same affection and care as Lord Krishna had been in the Dwapar Age which has been vividly described in Srimad Bhagavat Purana at great length."

"All the activities of this divine child were really celestial. The child was the source of delight to every beholder: to his age group he was a dear friend, to elders he was a sweet child. Following Mother Yashoda in the care of the child, Sumati did everything to keep her child happy. The child was not only precocious but had a very sharp brain. He learnt all education in no time. His wondrous achievements became the talk of the entire region. People used to throng at Vishnu Yasha's place to have even a fleeting glimpse of the child."

Vishnu Yasha had three sons named Kavi, Paragya and Sumantrak prior to Kalki's birth. All these three were god-fearing and they always respected the Brahmanas and their guru. They were all partial incarnations of Lord Supreme. The Brahmanas nourished and cared by the King Vishnu Yasha were the few of the nobles still left. Getting Lord Hari's Darshan they were very happy. As Kalki came of age Vishnu Yasha requested these Brahmanas to have his initiation ceremony (Yagyopaveeta Sanskaar) completed and that they must also arrange for his formal education. When the father asked Kalki to go for reading Veda, pretending his ignorance he casually asked: "O Sir! What are the Vedas? What is Savitri? And does he who learns this Sootra becomes cultured (Sanskaarita) to get the title of a Dwija?" In order to satisfy his son's queries the father said. "O Son! The Vedas constituted the real wisdom as they emerged from God's mouth. Savitri is the mother of Vedas. When a man learns the Vedas and their soul – the Savitni Sootra – he becomes a regular Brahmana. These Vedas stay with such Brahmanas only. I want to entrust you to these Brahmanas so that you be initiated formally into the sacred knowledge. I want you to become a Veda-versed Brahmana."

Having heard his father, Kalki further asked: "O Sire! What guided upbringing a Brahmana has? What are those rituals that make a Brahmana worship Lord Vishnu?" Then Vishnu Yasha enlightened his son on the duties of the Brahmana: Worshipping God at least thrice in a day (at every change: morning, evening and night), observing the Vedic rules and living ever in communion with Lord Almighty. This way such a Brahmana not only ensures peace in this life and the next but also the welfare of all beings. Such a Brahmana remains favourite of Lord Supreme. O Son! In this Kali Age those calumniators of Veda and Brahmana have started a campaign to negate all such holy teachings and they ever indulge in voilence against the noble persons. With the result, many such Brahmanas had to leave this country. And those who are left here have to compromise their values for bare survival. It is after seeing such distressing conditions of the world that the earth in the form of a cow accompanied the high deities to seek relief from Lord Almighty."

Hearing these painful words from his father, Kalki decided to take on this immoral age of Kali. But before that the Brahmanas initiated him and performed his sacred thread ceremony. Then Kali went to his guru's place to get the formal education. Seeing him so determined his father Vishnu Yasha felt reassured that now the terror of the iniquitous power would be squarely checked and the trend would be reversed.

While narrating the story of Kalki incarnation, Sootaji told Shaunak and other high sages that as soon as Sage Parashuram found Kalki ready for education he took him to his hermitage, situated atop the famous Mahendra Hill. While introducing himself, Sage Parashuram told Kalki: "I am son of Sage Jamadagni and Renuka. I know all the Shashtras, Vedas, Aagams and have been especially versed in the art of archery from times immemorial. I may tell you that it was I who slayed the thousand-armed Arjuna (Sahastraarjuna) and made the earth devoid of the tyrant Kshatriyas as many as twenty one times. I have repeatedly cleansed this earth for making it safe and conducive to the growth of Brahmanical values and for the strength of Dharma. You must accept me as your guru. O Brahman son, I shall grant you education and all relevant knowledge. This, my hermitage, is an ideal place to get education in and contemplate on the Vedic values of life. Whatever you wish to study here should be studied with utmost interest and concentration. Here you will not find any disturbance. The sweet chirping of the birds and peaceful atmosphere will help you read whatever you want to, with concentration. I shall grant you all sorts of learning so that you could take all the immoral and vile forces that are now seemingly overwhelming the world."

Guru Parashuram's reassuring exhortation made Kalki start his education in right earnest. Even though as Lord Hari be himself was the fount of all knowledge, in order to perform his worldly plays ('leela') with aplomb, he had to do so. So he started behaving like a normal human student. Continuing the narration, Sootaji said: "Thus with a resolute mind and enthusiastic heart Kalki completed his course in 64 arts, archery and others. Thus with his bowed head and bound hands he said to his guru Parashuram –" O my mentor and guide! Under your instruction I have completed my education. Now please tell me as to what fees I should offer to you for receiving this education. Please just indicate as to what I should do to discharge this obligation. Even otherwise I would try my best to put this learning to the best use in accordance with your wishes."

Hearing his disciple's gratifying words, Parashuram said, "O Lord! You are omniscient and knower of every heart's secret. But since, as my disciple, you have asked me about your course of action, I tell you this. The intention with which creator Brahma had supplicated for before Lord Hari in the company of other gods and earth has to be fulfilled by you. Your mission is destruction of the evil forces of this Kali Age. You have incarnated yourself in this form of Kalki for this basic purpose. Now having received all education and the secrets of marital arts from me by the grace of Lord Shiv, you must set out to achieve this objective. In order to be a full unit you must marry your eternal spouse already incarnate as the dughter of the King Vrihadrath of Sinhala Dweepa, Padma, first and then work for the re-establishment of the righteous order on this earth. When you take on and eliminate the infidels and tyrant kings with the help of the noble kings like Manu and Devapi, re-establish the righteous order as ordained in the Vedas, I will deem my fees as your mentor duly paid." Knowing this way about his education fees from his mentor and realising its importance, Kalki proceeded to Vilveshwar Mahadeva's temple and said his prayers. Having invoked Lord Shiv with a guileless heart, he said: "O Eternal Spouse of Uma, Lord of Universe, and always liberal to his devotees, I salute you and seek your eternal blessings. O Master of Yoga, you have incinerated Kaam's body will your Yoga fire. You are also the ruler of all evil spirits and the one responsible for the destruction of the vile forces of the earth and of those that have outlived their utility. I am quite aware of your illimitable powers and hence I seek protection under your grace." Lord Mahadeva, on hearing this feelingful prayer, appeared before him with his eternal spouse Uma and blessed Kalki in quite conformity with the divine norms. Blessing Kalki the Lord also said that he who chanted this way the hymns created by Kalki will have all his mortal fears scotched. Then he presented Kalki a unique Shuka (parrot), as fast moving as a sturdy steed, well versed in all knowledge, and asked his devotee to accept the bird reverentially. All this while Parvati stood rather bewildered. 'Why Lord be so gracious to a mere mortal?' she thought. Dispilling her confusion Lord Mahadeva further said, with an eye on his spouse's visage: "O Kalki! Now you are well versed in all human knowledge. You shall ever be a victor." Saying so and indicating his devotee's divine powers to suggest his being Lord Vishnu's incarnation, the Lord presented a unique sword, named Ratna Maru, which had no parallel in the entire world. "Hold this sword and be a success in your mission." Kalki thought as if his prayer to Lord Shiv had been answered. He immediately rode on that fast flying unique parrot with that divine sword in his hand and headed for his village Sambhal. After bowing to his parents, his elder brothers, he related all his experience in education and worship, hearing which all felt doubly reassured that the days of distress and disturbance were now surely numbered. When King Vishaakh Yoopraj heard about Kalki receiving education from Sage Parashuram and those rare gifts from Lord Shiv, he was convinced that Lord Hari had incarnated in the form of Kalki. Not only the king but all the noble persons of his kingdom, the Veda reading Brahmanas, holy men, righteous Kshatriyas, honest traders felt immensely relieved. This message made their hearts again optimistic and they felt as though they had received a new lease on their life. They all urged upon their willing ruler to go in their company to felicitate Kalki and express their glee at his commitment to wipe out the reign of terror and loot of Kaliyug. While talking to the king Kalki unveiled his concept of a model society: Brahmana studious and liberal-hearted, Kshatriyas brave and kind-hearted, Vaishyas god-fearing and honest and the Shoodras submissive and dutifully subservient. Bhagwan Kalki told him that after his birth he was finding the conditions quietly improving, adding: "O King! You must arrange for performing a huge sacrifice (Yagya) – whether the Raajsooya Yagya or the Ashwamedha Yagya." Then he made the king realise that he (Kalki) was 'All in all'; in all realms, all rewards and all actions. With his advent the dynasties of the Sun and Moon would be headed by the benign kings Devapi and Manu respectively and Satya Yuga in return would be expedited. "Until this happens I shall continue to strive for this end."

Having learnt this secret from Lord Hari's (Kalki's) own mouth, the god-fearing king, Raja Vishaakh Yoop was thrilled and bowed his head reverentially before the latest Incarnation. Then he prayed: "O Lord! Please enlighten me also on the five basic tenets of the Vaishnava Dharma"

Sootaji, while narrating this story to the huge assembly of the sages in Nemisharanya, retold whatever he had learnt from his mentor. Addressing King Vishaakh Yoop, Kalki Bhagwan said: "When completing its term the universe would be reduced back to the basic elements, the whole of it would, in fact, coalesce unto me only. Remember that it was only I who existed before this creation and I it is who shall exist after this creation is dissolved into the basic elements. I am the sole sustainer of this entire Existence and the very fount of all the deities including Brahma and others. Brahma is omniscient and the creator who creates in accordance with my instruction as enshrined in the Vedas. He created all beings, all materials including the illusive ones which are known as part of my Maya. It was in this process that Manu and Prajapatis were created. The Brahmanas are created with my partial powers. They keep me happy with their knowledge and ritualistic activities. They are the top creations of this universe and the best among all the castes. Since they deem this entire creation to be ever instinct with me, they stay in eternal communion with me."

Hearing these details the king wanted to know the very symptoms of a noble Brahmana. "Which is that feeling that keeps them eternally drawn to you?" Satisfying the king's queries, Kalki Bhagwan said: "Listen, O King! The Vedas are God which themselves are uttered by Brahmanas. The Vedas exhort every being to do one's assigned job. It is the Brahmana's noble conduct which reflects the essence of my bhakti (devotion). Hence I stay in communion with them because of their unflinching devotion to me. It is this bhakti of the noble which repeatedly draws me to this world. The scholars claim that if a Brahmana,[1] with totally pious devotion, follows the Vedas he becomes capable of invoking even Lord Almighty at will. This devotion is symbolically called the knot of the sootra (flow of thought, i.e., like a knot draws all the threads, the same way all thoughts get drawn to bhakti or devotion of God). The three sootras represent the three modes of life: 'Sato-guna', 'Rajo-guna', 'Tamo-guna' and knot is devotion to God. This knot is also Brahma Granthi (the celestial knot). It is this thread which is worn at the time of the Yagyapaveeta ceremony. It has three threads bound by a knot called the Brahma-Granthi. Those who deem Yajurveda to be their fount of learning wear this sac— d thread upon their left shoulder. No matter who wears thi-. sacred thread it should always be kept above the navel. A Brahmana must have his forehead marked with a Tripunda (three lined mark) made from pious soil, ash and sandal paste. Each of the line of the mark ought to be of one finger's breadth. It is believed that the holy mark's three prongs represent Brahma, Vishnu and Mahesh. This mark adds to the glory of the Brahmana."

"The heaven is placed (symbolically) in the hand of the Brahmanas with Lord Vishnu having his abode therein. A Brahmana's voice perfects Veda chanting and their bodies have all the piety of the holy tirthas. His nerves contain the essential parts of the three basic natures (Satvika, Rajas and Tamas). Similarly, O King, a pure Brahmana ritually doing his worship activities has Savitri staying in his throat.

---

1.   Here the term 'Brahmana' encapsulates all noble beings.

Brahma resides at his heart and in the centre of his bosom the Dharma in its essential form. Behind this Dharma resides adharma. O King Vishaakh Yoop! Those who know the very essence of the four-caste-system are these Veda-reading Brahmanas only. I love a Brahmana who is resolute in his action, learned and innocent like a child. My protecting hand always stays over them. I harken to their succour unfailingly and incarnate myself wherever they need me. This glory of the noble Brahmanas is capable of destroying all the afflictions of this Kali Yuga." Having heard all about the tenets of the Vaishnavi faith and the glory of the noble Brahmanas, king Vishaakh Yoop returned happily to his kingdom."

When the king was gone, the parrot given to Kalki by Lord Shiv came near Kalki and it started hymning him with great feeling. Having heard the hymn, Kalki asked the parrot: "O Shuka! Where are you coming from now? What sort of food did you have today?"

The Shuka (parrot) replied: "O Lord! Whatever I have witnessed today is quite extraordinary. You will also be surprised when you learn about it. Today, flying merrily, I happened to come above the Sinhala Dweep situated amidst the ocean. There what had happened, I give you the details."

"King Vrihadrath rules over Sinhala Dweep. He has a daughter whose character is as pious and pure as nectar. Sinhala Dweep has all the four castes: Brahmana, Kshatriya, Vaishya and Shoodra dwelling in happily. The daughter took birth from the womb of the King's queen. The entire Sinhala Dweep is very picturesque and a beautiful place to dwell in. It has many huge palaces made of gold, silver and costly gems. There the women are extremely beautiful and they wear very attractive clothes. The palaces are surrounded with very picturesque ponds in which the birds frolic with gay abandon. The flower bees buzz very sonorously. King Vrihadrath is a very mighty and chivalrous ruler. His daughter Padmavati is renowned for her beauty and charms."

Then dwelling on the head-to-toe beauty description of the girl, Shuka said: "Her face is very attractive. That high charactered girl can spellbind even Kaamdeva's wife Rati. Perhaps she is incomparable in her beauty all over the world. It is believed that she is the incarnation of Goddess Lakshmi. Like Goddess Parvati, she remains engaged in the worship of God to get the desired husband. It is said that once Lord Shiva and Goddess Gauri had gone to Sinhala Dweep for giving their Darshan to that incomparable girl. She was somewhat shyful seeing the eternal couple before her. As she was too stunned to find her chosen couple before her, it was to propitiate them that she did this worship. Then Lord Shiv also blessed her that soon she would get her desired groom who shall be Lord Hari himself as no lesser being could even think of marrying her."

Lord Shiv also said: "In case any mortal being, driven by lust, dares to cast a foul eye at her he would become instantly a woman. The same shall be the fate of any being from the categories of divinities, Daitya (giants), Gandharva, Yaksha or Kinnars as the exclusive right of being her husband reserves with Lord Hari only.

Then, advising her the Lord said: "O Girl! Now you must shed off this frugal tic life pattern and start enjoying life in full as soon your desires shall be fulfilled." Blessing her thus, the eternal couple (Gauri-Mahadeva) disappeared.

Padma or Padmini was pleasantly surprised to see the eternal couple blessing her this way. She was overwhelmed with joy and delight. She felt supremely delighted at the prospect of getting Lord Hari as her husband. She got what she had been striving for all these years. Deeming her prayers answered she returned to the palace with her maids.

As she returned to the palace her charms became all the more appealing. Although for a mother of a comely daughter pride is a natural sentiment, yet at times it becomes a cause of worry as well. Her mother was worried lest she should fail to get a matching groom for her daughter. When after some time King Vrihadrath saw his daughter so fully blossomed with charms and beauty, he also became worried about her marriage. The King discussed with his Queen the matter concerning his daughter's marriage and asked her whether a Swayamvar should be arranged to make his daughter get the desired groom. The Queen, Kaumudi, well aware of her daughter receiving the boon from Lord Shankar, told her husband: "Lord! I have heard from Padma's friends about her receiving a boon from Lord Shankar according to which she is destined to get Lord Hari (Vishnu) as her husband. According to this divine scheme, no one else can get to this position. Should any one also try to get Padma as bride he would be instantly converted into a woman."

Getting this information King Vrihadrath was partially relieved of the trouble of getting her daughter a suitable groom but he was rather worried: "When would Lord Hari marry my daughter? Do I have such a fortune as to get Lord Hari as my son-in-law? Will I have to get the sea churned, as in the remote past, to provoke the Great Lord to expedite the process of His marraying Padma?"

Thus thinking, King Vrihadrath decided to hold the Swayamvar. He sent invitation to all the deserving kings and princes. In no time all of them began to gather in the Sinhala Dweepa with their retinue and other paraphernalia. Included among them were the famous rulers of the time as Ruchira, Suparna, Madiraksha, Krishnasaar, Parada, Jeemoota, Kroora- Mardan, Aash, Kushambu, Rank, Kathan, Sanjaya, Guru Mitra, Pramaani, Vijrambha, Srinjaya, Akshaya and many others of sturdy body and comely visage. Soon the royal court of Vrihadrath was filled to the capacity with the aspiring kings and princes. All of them were bedecked in their most flaunting royal dresses and looking very attractive and enthusiastic. King Vrihadrath's staff was looking after their comforts.

Gradually, the well bedecked bride, Padma, entered the count flanked by her maids carrying the victory garland to be put round the neck of the selected groom. As she moved with measured steps she outsmarted even Kaam-deva's [the love-god's] wife Rati in her charms and manners.

Describing her beautious form, Shuka told Maharaj Kalki: "O Lord! I have been visiting all the high and low realms but I am yet to see any female excelling her charm and beauty anywhere. She looked every inch Goddess Lakshmi when she entered the royal court."

Continuing the narration, Sootaji told the seers assembled in the holy tirtha of Nemisharanya. "The roayl court of Vrihadrath looked as graceful as Maharaja Janaka's court might have looked at the time of Sita's Swayamwar. As she moved on, tinkling her anklets the assembled kings and princes felt ensnared by her incomparable charm. Smiling shyly and spreading her charms, she appeared Beauty personified, as it were. All the kings fell for her and they began to look at her with a sensual charge. As they did so, vindicating Lord Shiv's boon to princess Padma, they kept on getting converted into female beings. With the result, an unusual scene began to emerge there: the princess Padma leading the group of her maids, followed by many kings and princes who had become female owing to their casting their covetous eye at the princess. Seeing this, Padma felt worried: "What would happen now? If Lord Hari doesn't care to come to me, my father's insistence would convert all the kings and princes of this earth into females." Sensing her worry her friend asked of the cause and the princess said: "It appears as though Lord Shankar's boon is failing. Lord Hari is not here and there is no indication of his coming here either. Even though he learns about my ardent wish of marrying him, will be ever agree? And should he really refuse then my entire penance would go waste as that of sowing an unfertilisable seed into the land of my desires. Now I take a vow. In case he (Lord Hari) fails to grant my desire, I shall incinerate my body through the raging fire in his memory only."

Telling Kalki Maharaja of Padma's burning agony, Shuka (the parrot) told her: "O Lord, seated on a tree close by the chamber I heard her and I was thawed with sympathy. I thought it to be my foremost duty to apprise you of these pathetic tidings. Hence I am here telling you all about her."

Whereupon Lord Hari (Kalki) said to the parrot: " O Shuka! In order to reassure Padma on my behalf you will have to go again to Sinhala Dweep. There is no doubt that she is my bride and I shall marry her. Go and give my message to her. Tell her about me and my resolve to marry her only. Lord Shankar's word cannot be belied. This is her destiny and I must honour it. O Shuka! You are very wise and learned. You must impress upon the princess that her destiny would have her marrying me. Assure her that soon I'd come and marry her. Then you must quickly report back to me."

Getting this responsibility entrusted by Bhagwan Kalki, and deeming its efforts bearing the desired fruits, the parrot speedily headed towards Sinhala Dweep again. It crossed the ocean flying and took bath in a pond. Then it had its meal of citrous fruits and straightaway entered the royal palace. Getting in to the princess's chamber, it perched itself atop the tree of Nagakesara and accosted the princess: "O beloved of Vishnu, with such a comely stature and enchanting face! May your welfare remain ever assured. You can ensnare the whole world by your charms. Lord Almighty has liberally endowed you with very captivating charms."

Delighted to hear the parrot speaking so enchantingly, she said: "O Shuka Devata! Who, actually, are you? Are you a god or a demon in the form of a parrot? Why are you showering so much of affection on me? You appear to be my well-wisher. But, beware, lest you fall for me sexually and turn into a female parrot also !"

Getting this light banter-filled remark and detecting her impatience, Shuka said: "O Devi! I know all the arts and sciences as well as all the scriptures. I can move anywhere in the universe. I have come here deeming you to be troubled by your agony. For no rhyme or reason you have discarded the beautiful clothes and ornaments. What is the reason behind your feeling so lost and distressed right in the peak of your youth? Yours is an age of making merry and enjoying life. You are such a girl whose mere utterance can delight an aspirant of beauty and complete fruitfully her ambition. How come you feel so much wane and disheartened? Tell me the cause of your trouble. May be, I can be of some help to you. Deem me as your guileless well wisher and open out your heart before me."

Finding such an encouraging, learned and responsible advisor in the form of a parrot, Padma said: "O Shuka! The greatest misfortune is God seemingly working against me. Because even if you are born in a noble royal family, well endowed with beauty and brains, the moment God turns against you all these attributes and virtues are of just no avail. Perhaps you don't know about my life. Right since my childhood to adulthood, I performed a great penance to get my beloved Lord as husband. I had prayed hard to Lord Shankar who, with his spouse, did appear before me. Then the Lord had asked me to get my boon. But shyness kept my lips sealed. However, reading my wish the Lord had said that

Lord Vishnu would be my husband. He also told me that should any man, god, demon or other sub-divine species' male being demand me as his wife, he shall turn into a female immediately! Giving this boon Lord Shiv had also instructed me in the formal worship of Lord Vishnu which I performed ever with full devotion. But still I am to meet my Lord! All of these female maids that surround me are, actually, kings and princes who looked at me with amorous intention. They had all turned up in my Swayamvar but this is what they have been reduced to. Although even my father knows that I am destined to get Lord Vishnu as my husband, yet it appears we are not that much fortunate. When he got no hint about the Lord coming to seek my hand, he had the Swayamvar organized to discharge his paternal duty. But even then Lord Vishnu didn't shower his grace. Meanwhile, all my prospective (could-have-been) grooms had become female. Now in my company they are together engaged in propitiating Lord Vishnu to regain their male form as only he can overrule the boon of Lord Shiv. But neither has he come nor shown any indication to expect his arrival."

Whereupon, Shuka asked: "O fair one ! Would you please tell me in details the method of formal Vishnu worship that you were instructed about and which you practised all this while? You are indeed very blessed as Lord Shiv himself instructed you about it. Now I am fortunate enough to learn it from you. I hope when I learn of that method, by grace of God I may also get a better species after I quit my present mortal coil. Moreover, this worship may nullify all the consequences of my evil deeds done earlier and assure a nice realm after my death."

Hearing such a feelingful request, Padma said: "This method of worshipping Vishnu, as detailed out to me by no one else but Lord Shakar, is very meritoious—fruit-giving itself. Learning this automatically removes all the stigmas that the listener has attached to his name – including even the murder of a cow or Brahmana and spreading blasphemy. Now listen it carefully: In it the Strotra (hymn) 'OM NAMO NARAYAN SWAAHAA' has great importance. The aspirant, first of all, takes bath early in the morning, preferably at dawn, and after thoroughly cleaning himself (or herself) takes seat on a Kusha-asana. Then arrange the things of worship in accordance with the Vedic instructions and concentrate deeply on Lord Vishnu's visage. Then while offering oblation etc., one should perform the worship – first bathing the Lord's emblem in cow's five products (Panchagavya). Cleaning it and redecorating it on the exalted seat and then saying the prayer after offering oblation – while constantly chaning the mantra told before. Those who do with full devotion have their all wishes fulfilled. Finally closing the worship with the humble submission to the Lord – I seek shelter under thy shade – the performer should distribute the remainder of the oblation as the 'Prasadam'. The conclusion of the Pooja should be extended with all prayers one knows of his or her chosen Lord. [Then she tells about one such prayer with detailed description of the chosen Lord as given below in translation.]

"He whose sole is marked with holy circles, whose anklets sound like the billed ankle rings, whose yellow raiment gives the impression of a flowing flag, whose huge arms cover the whole universe – which have also crushed many a tyrant demons – I ever concentrate my mind on to his virage. [This way Lord Hari's Body's each part is praised and prayed for in superlative terms]. Concluding her narration Padmavati said: "O Shuka! He who performs this kind of worship everyday has his or her all desires fulfilled. Those who do so are blessed as their all evil deeds get nullified and the good deeds tremendously magnified to improve their lot in this world and in the next."

2
Marriage And Early Encounter With Evil Forces

Continuing the narration Sootaji told the high sages in Nemisharanya that the messenger of Kalki, Shuka, of great determination and knowledge, said to· Padma sitting amidst her female friends, "O Devi, almost the replica of Goddess Lakshmi, may your wish be fulfilled. You have obliged me greatly by telling in details the method of ritual worship of Vishnu as instructed to you by Lord Mahadeva. Since the time you told me this sin-destroying and salvation-ensuring method of Lord Vishnu's worship I have been almost visualising the grand form of Lord Vishnu with you as his spouse. But in that vision I also see a person dwelling across the ocean, and having all the attributes of Lord Vishnu. I find no difference in him and Lord Vishnu."

Hearing Shuka's remark, Padma was pleasantly surprised and felt greatly enthusiastic to learn more about such a man existing on the earth. "Is he the real incarnation of Lord Vishnu? If you tell me more details about that person I would treat you very lavishly. I will have your beak plated with gold and head with an ornate, gem-embedded diadem. I will have your wings painted with holy vermilion power and your neck bedecked with the Suryakanta gem. I will also tie sweetly tingling anklets so that wherever you go, you make the atmosphere sonorous. The nectar oozed out by your talks has quelled all the agitation I was feeling in my heart and has given me a ray of fresh hope. Also, you must instruct me as to what should I do further to honour you, my trouble-shooter."

Hearing Padma's sweet words that parrot left the tree and flew to the princess' vicinity and said: "O Devi! Lord Hari has incarnated himself again in the house of the Brahmana

Vishnu Yasha – as his son – of the village Sambhal for re-establishing the rule of the moral law (Dharma) and for causing the decline in immoral values. Before his incarnation Vishnu Yasha had three elder sons. This incarnation has come to be known as Kalki Avataar. Now the Lord resides there in the village Sambhal with his parents and brothers. After his sacred thread ceremony he went to Sage Parashuram to get complete education in all arts and sciences including the martial arts and archery. He had received from Lord Shiv a lovely steed, a sword, a parrot (Shuka himself) armour and the blessing to rid the world of the iniquitous tyrants. As he returned home, the news of his prowess in all arts, sciences and martial arts reached the ears of Raja Vishaakh Yoop, the ruler of the region. The king personally came there to pay his regard to Bhagwan Kalki. Looking at the king's devotion and guileless heart, Kalki narrated many instances from the scriptures to dispel whatever doubts he had. Since then he is happily staying in that village Sambhal."

Getting these details from the parrot, the princess was very happy. She developed a surging wave of hope. Begging and beseeching of the parrot to go and bring Bhagwan Kalki there with due honour, she presented the bird with all the gifts that she had promised. Then she said: "O Shuka! What more should I tell you as you know everything that I aspire for? But owing to being a girl I am rather apprehensive, naturally. In case Lord Kalki doesn't agree to come here, you must request him on my behalf this way: Lord Shiv had given me a boon that only Lord Hari – that is your good honoured self – is capable in marrying me. Should anyone want to marry me that being is sure to become a female, no matter he be from the gods, man, demons or even gandharva's category. My father, by organising a Swayamvar for my marriage, has seen the consequential effect of this boon. All the invited kings and princes have turned female. Now all of them are my female companions. So, in case he doesn't marry me, Lord Shiv's boon shall turn into a worst curse for me. Hence in order to save my life, Lord Kalki must come here to marry me." Hearing this request the parrot bowed his head to Princess Padma and speedily flew away to Sambhal village.

That parrot, reaching the destination, went straight to Lord Kalki who was surprised to see his favourite messenger so very well bedecked with gold ornaments. The brilliant being (Lord Kalki) welcomed his pet parrot and, feeding the bird on milk, asked: "O Shuka! I am amazed to find you so very well decked with gold ornaments and so well looked after. Which country are you coming from? Who have you met to look so cheerful? You have been far away so long. You know how I miss you when you are not near me. Tell me in details all about your absence for such a long period."

Shuka, touched by Lord Kalki's affection, replied: "O Lord! I have been doing something for the general welfare of the world." Then he revealed all the details of its meeting with Padmavati and her problem. Concluding, he said: "O Lord! It appears to be an inkling of the destiny that you marry that incomparable girl blessed by Lord Mahadeva specifically for this purpose only." As Kalki heard these details, he rode upon his horse and accompanying Shuka left for Sinhala Dweep that very moment.

While flying above Maharaj Kalki saw the high rise buildings, huge palaces, ponds, parks etc. of that city of Sinhala Dweep. He was quite impressed by the affluence of the region and its natural beauty. The capital city of Simhala Pradesh was Karumati. He was delighted to find the palace of Padma surrounded with cooling, flower filled ponds having chirping geese frolicking. The palace was covered with myriad trees of natural elegance and fragrance. Seeing one pond very tempting, Kalki said to Shuka: "O Shuka! I want to take bath in this pond." "Oh! Very well, Sir!" So saying and leaving Kalki Bhagwan to have his bath he straightaway left for Princess Padma's private chamber. The bird then gave the happy news to the princess about Lord Kalki's arrival. Padma suddenly found Nature very pleasing with cool breeze disturbing her raiments. Shuka's reassuring words appeared to Padma as the soothing balm. "Oh.... dear Shuka! I am so glad you have come with this great news. May God ensure your welfare eternally." Shuka said to the princess. "O fair Dame! By your prayers and noble intentions I have my welfare assured in every way."

Padma said: "O Shuka! In your absence, disturbed by a variety of apprehensions I was getting very much nervous and agitated. "Rest assured," butted in the bird, "the moment you behold Bhagwan Kalki all your apprehensions would be quelled. His Darshan will act as a soothing balm for you."

Whereupon Padma said: "Will I ever be fortunate enough to have his Darhshan? Am I that blessed?" "Worry not, O princess! Now your bad days stay numbered. O desirous of having the unique groom, your wish is about to be fulfilled. My Lord, Kalki Bhagwan has come. He is staying near the lotus pond close to your palace. In fact, I came here first to give this happy news to you."

Padma was thrilled, she looked at Shuka with his gratitude filled eyes. The she said: "In order to have water plays I am going that side with these eight female friends. They are Vimala, Malini, Leela, Kamla, Kaam Kanjala, Vilasini, Charumati and Kumuda." Saying so she asked her friends to have her royal palanquin ready.

Exactly like Rukmini had employed the trick to meet Lord Krishna before marriage and to get eloped by him was what Padma also had in her mind. The way her palanquin was being carried on became deserted in no time because in the fear of becoming female all the male citizens had withdrawn to their homes. Accompanying the palanquin were Padma's eight friends subduedly singing gratulatory songs, hearing which the birds also started chirping gleefully. As they reached near the pond, they started to have their bath. After taking bath in the scented water they all, including Padma, emerged with such an enchanting radiance of their beauty that even the flower bees started rapaciously budging around them. Having readied herself Padmavati headed with her friends to that Kadamb tree beneath which Lord Kalki was drowsing. Even from a distance he gave the impression as though the veritable sun was relaxing under that tree. His body glow was out witting thousands of Kaam-Devas. Princess Padma saw his grand stature: bluish, radiant body clad in the Pitambar (yellow raiment) with red lotus like eyes partially closed. The gem of Kaustubh looked graceful on his bosom. Beholding that incomparably handsome youth, Padmavati was spellbound and stunned in the awe of that personality. She was so much overwhelmed by that ensnaring spectacle that she even forgot to ritually welcome him. Out of sheer coyness she thought it unwise to awaken him. Also, she had a fear in her mind: "Should he behold me with amorous intentions, he might turn into a female being? After all, it hasn't yet been confirmed that he is the incarnation of Lord Vishnu – my only possible groom by Lord Shiv's boon – and until this happens I am against taking any impetuous chances."

As if Lord Kalki had read what Padma's brain was thinking, He, the all-knowing super soul of this entire universe – the Omniscient Lord – all of a sudden came out of his slumber and opened up his eyes. He was surprised to behold a very beautiful and charming woman – identical to Lakshmi – standing before him. While gazing at her visage without blinking his eyes, Kalki accosted Padma: "O Kanta (beautiful woman)! Come closer. Your meeting appears to prove very auspicious for me. A mere glance at your face has seemingly evaporated all the languor and laziness that I felt due to journey – fatigue. O fickle! You have created a desire even in my placid heart. O beauteous girl! I am getting charged to get you merely by beholding you. Now I can get peace only when I have imbibed the nectar reposed in your soft lips. May your elephant trunk like soft hands and thighs get entwined around my body and quell its sexual agitation." This way Kalki Bhagwan started to poetically express the longings felt by his body and mind. Padma was delighted to find Kalki having so virile a body that didn't change its sex at the longing expressed by it – thus confirming what Lord Shiv had asserted in his boon to her. Now she realised that Lord Shiv's boon was really a boon and not a curse. This further confirmed Kalki to have been the incarnation of Lord Vishnu only. Padma felt greatly reassured.

While narrating this incident Sootaji told the assembly of the high sages that seeing the boon given by Lord Shiv about to vindicate itself, Padma began to hymn Kalki Maharaj: "O Lord of this creation, O Spouse of Goddess Lakshmi! Now I have identified you. Now you must protect me every way as I seek your shelter. Indeed I am really blessed that I could have you before me. It is the result of the noble and meritorious deeds I performed that I could behold your lotus feet so close to me. O Provider of the succour from distress, O Protector of the righteous rule, please allow me touching your lotus feet and going home to inform all others about your arrival that pleases everybody."

Saying so and touching his feet, Padma left for her palace to tell her father in details about the happy tidings. King Vrihadrath, getting from Padma's female friends the hint about his daughter's eagerness to marry Kalki, felt greatly relieved. Then the King invited his priests, bards and the gratulatory-song-singing-maids to accompany him and left for escorting Kali formally to his palace and welcome him ceremonially.

At the royal command Karumati city was decorated like a comely bride to welcome the most honoured guest. As King Vrihadrath reached the pond, he saw from a distance the Incarnation, Maharaj Kalki, seated on a jewel embedded high perched seat. His blue complexioned body beshone from the lustre of his gold ornaments as though dark clouds look bright when lightning strikes. Seeing him well decorated with a yellow raiment covering his entire body, the king was wonder-struck with awe and delight. Having formally worshipped and honoured him, the king accosted Kalki Maharaj in very reverential terms the following manner: "O Lord, as Yadunath had met Mandhata's son in the jungles, so you have met me here to bless my life." With great regard he ceremoniously welcomed him and escorted him back to his place. There the honoured guest was lodged in the best chamber of the palace. The King then formally betrothed his daughter with the ceremonial 'donation' of his daughter. The lotus-born Brahma arranged the marriage of the lotus-like Padma to the lotus-eyed Lord Hari. The King then gave a huge dowry in marriage. Getting the most desirous bride, Kalki Maharaja was gratified. He also gave liberally to the nobles and Brahmanas as their due and stayed for some time in Sinhala Dweep in the company of his newly wed bride.

All the kings who had turned female when they expressed their intention of marrying Padma – by Lord Shiv's boon to the princess – also assembled there to worship the Lord Hari. By dint of their Darshan of the Lord they also regained their lost manhood after, by Lord's grace, they touched his feet and took bath in the river Rewa flowing close by. Although Padma and Kalki had starkly contrasting body complexions, Padma was clad in the blue raiments and Kalki in yellow to maintain their stark contrast. Collectively they gave a radiance of the reddish hue which appeared very charming to all the persons assembled there.

When they got their lost manhood, all the kings assembled round Lord Kalki to hymn him in utter reverence and gratitude. "Victory to thee! O Lord of the world! It is your instinctive power which creates this entire world. After the Pralaya, the entire universe gets coalesced in your form in the elemental stage. You always incarnate yourself whenever there is distress to the noble values and righteous conduct in this creation. When the divine army, led by Indra, was defeated and the three realms' victor Hiranyaksha decided to slay Indra, it was you who became incarnate as Lord Varaha (Boar) to rescue the gods and re-establish this world on its even keel. During the Great Churning, when the gods and the demons failed to find a solid support to base their churner at, you assumed the form of the Koorma (Tortoise) to solve their problem and had the ocean properly churned. When the gods were distressed by Hiranyakashyapu, you appeared as Nri-Singh (Man-Lion) to tear apart that tyrant demon lord and save life of your pet devotee, Prahlad.

"When Bali, the demon-lord, organised a Yagya with the intention of ruling over the entire world, you assumed the form of Vaman (Dwarf) to fail his scheme and in the process you managed to force the king donate all the three realms to you. When the kings and princes of the Haihaya Dynasty grew iniquitously tyrant, flouting all norms of propriety, you assumed the form of Parashuram, a scion of sage Bhrigu's lineage to cause their doom. In order to cleanse the earth of the blood-thirty tyrant Kshatriyas – when they tried to steal away sage Jamadagni's cow – you rooted them out as many as twenty-one times."

"It was you, O Lord, who had also slayed Ravan, the son of Vishrawa, in your seventh incarnation as Lord Rama. In order to set right the rule of propriety, you had taken birth in the Raghu's dynasty, as the son of Dashrath. Receiving education from Vishwamitra, the great sage, and marrying Sita by his design, you had to go in exile along with your brother Lakshman and wife Sita. There Sita was abducted by Ravan, the mighty father of Indra- trouncer, Indrajit. But undaunted, you could gather an army of apes to go to Ravan's citadel, Lanka, to kill the demon lord and secure Sita's release. Then you were born in Dwapar Age in Yadu's dynasty as

Krishna, son of Nanda. You had protected the rightful claim of all the distressed persons including the Pandavas and killed scores of tyrant kings and princes in the process. It was by your guidance that an usurper of his cousin's property, Duryodhan, was destroyed. At that time also your another incarnation had taken place as Balabhadra. Subsequently when the Brahma's ordained rule of order started going topsy-turuy, you incarnated as Buddha also."

"And in this age, you, the ruler of the three realms, have incarnated as Kalki to get rid of the alien rule – comprising of the followers of the Buddha and the Mlechchhas – and establish the Vedic rule once again. O Lord! You have also redeemed all of us from the curse of Lord Shiv to Padma and restored us our manliness. How can we describe your glory? We have no words. We, who feel unsettled merely at viewing a comely woman and thus always agitated, mortal beings, could see your lotus-feet by your grace only. We pray you to set right the topsy-turvy Vedic rule and re-establish in its pristine glory. Oblige us again O Lord !" – So saying the group of the kings broke into a whimper.

While telling all about Kalki's incarnation Sootaji said that then Lord Kalki dwelt upon the righteous conduct for each of the castes. The kings were greatly enlightened by his discourse. They bowed to him a hundred times and said "O Lord! How do men and women get rid of this cycle of life and death? What causes the body to grow, pass childhood, enjoy youth, bear through the old age and eventually die?"

Hearing this pithy question, Lord Kalki invoked Ananta Muni, a great sage dwelling for an infinite period in the holy spot. Deeming the call of Lord Kalki to be something which might grant him salvation, he immediately appeared before Kalki Lord. "Tell me, Lord, whatever I should do and wherever I should go?" Replying with a smile Kalki said: "O Great Sage, you have seen and analysed all the deeds that I have performed on the mortal plane. Nobody can nullify one's destiny and without action no fruit could be enjoyed." Hearing this the delighted sage began to get away. Seeing the sage departing the nervous kings supplicated before the Great Lord: "O Lord? What did you ask the sage and what was his response? Most unusual. What was the object of your discussion with him? Please enlighten us with details."

Detecting the great curiosity in the kings' request Lord Kalki replied: "Well, detailed answer to these questions be only given by the sage, Ananta, the man with a placid heart." Thereupon the kings asked the sage: "O Great Soul! What was the object of your discussion with Lord Kalki? We couldn't decipher this and we eagerly want to know about it."

This made the sage start his narration with a story. "In olden times in the city called Purika, there dwelled a learned Vedic scholar. He was, actualy, my father. But, despite being a man, I was impotent. My father's name was Vidrun, and mother's Soma. My physical debility was the sole thorn of flesh in my parents' life. Even physically I had no good features either. Distressed with my unblessed existence, my father decided to stay in a jungle in lonliness and worship Lord Shiv devotedly and with full rituals. "Hymn him", he said, "Lord Shiv, the Master of the three realms and the last refuge of all mortal existences. Serpent Vasuki keeps your neck covered while Ganga reposes herself in your dense locks. I bow to you, O fount of all blessings! Propitiated easily, the instantly propitiable god appeared before my father, astride his bull and asked my father to get his boon. Then Vidrun, my father, requested my becoming a potent male as any other man. Lord Mahadeva, flanked by his spouse Parvati, accepted the request."

When he returned home from the jungle after his penance he was delighted to see me sexually potent again. Soon he got me married. After my marriage I was extremely happy and devoted myself exclusively in loving my bride. After some time my parents expired. I religiously performed their last rites and fed the holy Brahmans in their obsequies ceremony. Since I loved my parents dearly, their demise made me lonely and forlorn. I devoted myself to Lord Vishnu's worship. Propitiated with my deep and devoted worship Lord Vishnu explained during my sleep (in dream) that 'verily affection and love are also part of my illusive plays (Maya). It is affection for the dear ones that keeps the mind agitated which in turn causes the body to age. Do not treat them as the final truths.' When I was about to argue with the Lord, he disappeared and my sleep was also broken. Immediately I took my wife along to leave that Purika City in order to weaken the bonds of past affection, and visiting the few holy spots devoted to Lord Vishnu, I went and settled with my family and followers in deep south. Then I again immersed myself to Lord Vishnu's worship.

"Dwelling there while worshipping Lord Vishnu as many as twelve years passed. One day when I was taking bath in the sea, I was so trapped in the billowing wave of the ocean that I couldn't even get up. Seeing me lying so forlorn the aquatic beasts began to trouble me. This disturbance agitated my mind as much as to make me feel forlorn and full of despair. I didn't know when the slap of one billowing sea wave made me unconscious. The wave pushed me to the sea-shore. There I was espied by a noble Brahmana, Vridha Sharma who happened to pass from the spot I was lying at. He was kind enough to escort me to his home and began to look after me as though I was his own son.

"The sage Ananta, while telling the kings about his story, said that he was so lost in the new surroundings that he lost the sense of time and space. Resigning myself to the changed condition, I began to live there. Meanwhile deeming myself to be a Veda reading Brahmana, Vridha Sharma had solemnised my marriage with a comely girl. Getting her, a most deserving bride, I was amazed. She kept me fully occupied with her devoted service. Enjoying life to the full, I spent my time with her. From her I poduced five sons named Jai, Vijai, Kamal, Vimal and Budh. Thus I was living in the acme of comfort. This way I used to live like the divine chief, Indra. When my eldest son Jai came of age and grew nubile, a Brahmana called Dharmasaar offered his daughter in marriage to Jai. I happily accepted the proposal. Their marriage was duly solemnised under the guidance of the Veda versed Brahmanas. Having done so I thought of going to the sea-shore to offer my oblational tribute to the high sages and manes. As I emerged from the sea I saw that all my kith and kin from the earlier life were doing their evening (Sandhya) worship. Seeing them I was agitated a bit. I was surprised seeing their doing their worship to Lord Hari on a Dwadashi day. They also recognised me and finding no change in my form and appearance they said. "O Ananta ! You are a Vishnu devotee. What has agitated your mind so much? What have you seen? Please share your problems with us. I replied to them: "I have not seen anything but I do not know why have my senses become so much possessed with the feelings of the sexual urge. I feel as though the whole world is passing before me like a panorama of illusion."

All of a sudden I saw my previous wife Manini come rushing to me, crying: "O God! What is this? How come my husband has been reduced to such a pathetic condition?" But seeing my previous wife and the old relations of her in the company of the sages, I was further confused. Then, as my luck would have it, the supremely wise sage, Hansa Muni, happened to reach there to bless me with knowledge. All asked him as to what should be done to have me cured. Whereupon Paramhansa Muni, seeing me standing before him asked: "O Ananta! Why have you come here deserting your wife Charumati, Budh and other sons? Why have you left your native place as well? Don't you remember that today is the day of your son's marriage? But surprisingly I find you here, roaming at the sea-shore. There all religious people still miss you. I am also invited there. But you appear quite grief-stricken here. However, there you looked seventy years old but here you look hardly thirty. How is it?"

"Moreover, I didn't see your this wife there as well. Even I don't know how I have come here or who brought me here. I am not sure whether you are the same Ananta or someone else. Similarly I doubt whether I am the same beggar or other. My meeting you here gives the impression of an illusion. While you are a normal householder, I am an ascetic staying away from family, caring more for the next world and general welfare of the people. There appears to be the powerful influence of the illusion cast by Lord Hari's Maya whose reality could be realised only with the Advaita knowledge (the perception of 'non-difference' between the devotee and the deity) and not many normal understanding."

Continuing the narration, sage Ananta said only this much. Then he addressed sage Markandeya: "O Great Sage! Now I tell you something about a future happening. This Maya, of Tamasika nature, also gets its form from Lord Hari. Like a seasoned whore it draws every being's attention. No being is capable of destroying or even checking its over-powering effect. However, it gets destroyed at the beginning of Pralaya when nothing reigns but darkness, upon which perches Lord Hari. It is at the end of the period of Pralaya that the creator, Brahma, gets the inkling from Lord Hari to start the process of creation once again. He creates a male and female from his own body which leads to creation coming in its myriad forms along with the emergence of sense of ego and other attributes of life chiefly divided into three shades—Rajasika, Tamasika and Sathvika. But each and every being is affected by the unstoppable Maya. Those who are devoted to Lord Hari can only hope to get rid of this Maya. Once they realise the all-pervading from of Lord Harti, they get riddance from Maya's illusions to gain access to the Abode of Lord Supreme."

Recounting this story Shaunakji asked Sootaji: "O Brahman! What did the great Markandeya, Vashishtha, Vaamdeva and other high sages say hearing this story from sage Ananta?" Sootaji replied: "They were all delighted and wanted to listen to more about Maya and its overpowering influence upon beings."

Obliging the sages, the sage, Ananta, told his story which was listened to by even those kings and princes who had only recently regained their lost manhood: "O Kings! Whenever I tried to concentrate my mind on Lord Supreme it was frequently deviated by the thoughts of woman, son and wealth-property etc. This way I found myself frequently drawn to this illusive world. The moment I remembered my family, wealth, property etc., my soul again used to become restless. Failing repeatedly in my pursuits for peace I took a strong resolve to keep my senses under total control. When I did so, the presiding deities of the senses felt panicky. The ten deities ruling over the ten senses (five sensual perceptions and five intuitional ones) appeared before me to say "O Ananta! We are Disha, Vast, Pracheta, Ashwidwaya, Agni, Indra, Upendra and Mitra – the deities. We stay as the presiding deities of your senses. It is totally improper on your part to pierce your body with the edges of your nails to keep it subservient to your mind. This way you won't achieve your objective as excessive torture to your senses might even cause your death. We advise you, O Ananta, that if you really want to control your mind, fix it on to Lord Hari only. Because devotion to Lord Hari is entirely bliss-giving and liberation-ensuring as well. This devotion provides the best solace to the devotee. Only when you do so, you will get the Darshana of Lord Kalki to get eventual Moksha."

Continuing his recitation Ananta told the kings that it was for getting the Darshana of Kalki god that he had come there. I got the Darshana of that Formless One reaching here only. I became truly blessed getting his Darhsan which is the singular achievement of my life."

Saying so, sage Ananta, whose eye-lids gave the impression of lotus leaves, left after having the Darhsan of Padma's husband, Lord Kalki. Getting the direction the kings present there followed suit and got the salvation as sage Ananta had obtained.

Telling about it, Sootaji further said that when all the kings left, Lord Kalki decided to go back to his native place from Sinhala Dweep with his entourage and his wife Padma. When Indra, the divine chief, learnt about Lord Kalki's intention, he summoned the divine architect, Vishwakarma, and ordered him thus: "You should immediately go to Sambhal Gram (Village) and build beautiful palaces, ornate buildings, flower-laden ponds so as to show the best display of your art." Getting this order Vishwakarma was delighted and left for Sambhal. And before Lord Kalki could come to his native place with his bride he wrought extremely beautiful buildings and palaces for the Lord's stay. He created many houses designed on the shape of Garuda, Hamsa, and equipped them with all the arrangements for winters, summers and rainy season's comforts. Sambhal village looked as enchanting and beautiful as the capital of gods the city of Amaravati.

Meanwhile, accompanied by his wife Padma and his entourage, Lord Kalki came out of the city of Karunati, the capital of Sinhala Dweep, reached the sea-shore. Raja Vrihadrath, accompanied by his wife Kaumudi, also escorted them. While bidding good-bye to his daughter, the king was full of tears out of affection for his darling daughter. In dowry he gave to his daughter's husband 10,000 elephants, 100000 horses, 2000 chariots, 200 maids and uncountable ornaments, raiments and other gifts.

Thus formally sending his daughter to her in-law's place, Vrihadrath returned to his capital city and seeking blessings from his in-laws, Lord Kalki took bath in the ocean. While he was having bath he saw a jackal moving on the placid water surface and went across the sea. Lord Kalki followed suit and reached on the other shore of the ocean along with his entire army, entourage and bride, Padma. Reaching there he instructed Shuka, "O Shuka, you must now go to Sambhal and inform them of our arrival."

Shuka immediately flew to Sambhalpura village which was hardly recognisable even for Shuka. It had undergone a tremendous transformation. It had huge palatial houses, ornate with guns and jewels, and beautifully laid gardens and ponds replete with variegated birds. Cool breeze was blowing and that village stretching to seven Yojanas (about 14 miles) and beating even the divine city of Amaravati hollow with its grandeur and gaiety. Shuka was delighted to be there for many hours. It kept on savouring the delight and decor of the city, hopping from one tree to another in uncontrollable ecstasy and telling the listeners all that had transpired in Sinhala Dweep with great detail. As Lord Kalki's father, Vishnu Yasha, heard about these happy lidings he was beyond himself with ecastasy and gratitude for the divine favour he received: Then he passed on this message to King Vishaakh Yoop and his people who thronged the city to welcome the divine couple: Lord Kalki and his bride, Padma.

The village Sambhal, then, began to be decorated for the grandiose welcome to Lord Kalki. The whole region was sprinkled with sandal powder-mixed water kept in the golden pitchers. Huge banners, festoons were hung all over the place and the region looked supremely enchanting. The ladies burst into holy, guatulatory songs as Lord Kalki with Padma entered the place. Very reverentially they touched the feet of their parents who were enthralled receiving Padma as the bride of their beloved son. Padma was besides herself with quiet delight at getting such considerate parents-in-law and family. For many years Kalki dwelt there with his wife. His brother Kavi's wife bore two sons for her husband, named Vrihad Keerti and Vrihadbahu. Also, another brother Praagya's wife Sumuti produced two sons named Yagya and Vigya, while Sumat's wife, Maalini, bore two sons called Shasan and Vegavaan. Both the sons were very god-fearing and noble.

Meanwhile, staying at the village Sambhal Lord Kalki got two sons from his wife Padma, who were named Jai and Vijai. They were very powerful and had earned great renown in all the three realms. While staying there Lord Kalki detected his father's inclination to perform the Ashwamedha Yagya. He assured his father that soon he (Lord Kalki) would win over the lords of direction to perform the Yagya with great fanfare. With this assurance he touched his father's feet and left on his victory expedition. His first target was Keekatpur. It was a stronghold of the followers of the Buddha. The dwellers didn't follow the Vedic Rules, nor they offered oblation to the manes. They had no faith even in the next world's significance. They believed that whatever existed was this life only. Epicurean and hedonist by taste and temperament they believed only in eating and drinking, unmindful of the consequences of their deeds. The king of Keekatpur heard about Lord Kalki's arrival with the intention of waging the war against the infidels of the faith. He also collected two Akshohini strong army and came out of the city to defend.

Continuing the narration, Sootaji said: "The way a lion attacks the herd of elephants the same way Lord Kalki attacked that king's forces. Soon the followers of the Buddha began to flee. Seeing them pulverised Kalkiji challenged them: "Hey you Buddha followers. Don't run away. Face my forces to show your valour." Hearing this challenge thrown by Lord Kalki, the king, called Raja Jin, who had almost exhausted his strength, came before him with a sword in his hand. He fought very bravely and chivalrously which surprised even the divine onlookers. He even cast such a spell that he could captivate Lord Kalki but soon Lord Kalki reduced to smithereens his all weapons. The king, Vishaakh Yoop, who was also fighting with Lord Kalki, immediately wounded the enemy king, Raja Jin, who fell unconscious. Then Vishaakh Yoop was trounced by Raja Jin which also made Lord Kalki unconscious. Lord Kalki fell unconscious out of his own created sportive play. As he regained consciousness, Lord Kalki got down from Raja Vishaakh Yoop's chariot and reached before Raja Jin. Lord Kalki's horse, who was wounded by Raja Jin, became furious and started crushing the enemy forces under his feet. Meanwhile, Lord Kalki's lieutenant, Gargya, destroyed as many as ten thousand enemy soldiers. Kavi and his sons also slayed twenty thousand enemy soldiers. While the fight was continuing, Lord Kalki stood before Raja Jin and broke his back with a mighty kick. Raja Jin fell on to the ground. Seeing him getting defeated his forces began to flee in panic. The entire Buddhist forces were dazed with fright and nervousness. Seeing his brother falling on to the ground, Shuddhodan, the brother of Raja Jin, came before Lord Kalki to avenge for his brother's fall. As Kavi saw Shuddhodan approach Lord Kalki, from his seat atop an elephant he shot a volley of arrows to hurt Shuddhodan severely. Now a hair-raising duel ensued between Kavi and Shuddhodan. Making dreadful sound they started to cast severe mace-blows upon each other. All of a sudden, casting his mace blow with a roaring charge Kavi made Shuddhodan fall. Then he cast a massive blow with his heel on to his heart. Although Shuddhodan fell, immediately, he stood up and cast a massive blow with his mace at Kavi. Despite Kavi losing his consciousness, he didn't lose his balance and stood erect. This surprised many.

However, when Shuddhodan found the enemy very powerful he left in his chariot to pray the Goddess Maya so that she could cast her black magic spell. Assisted by Mayadevi's powers Shuddhodan reached the battle field again with his million strong army. The chariot he was riding was also having the image of the goddess surrounded by a variety of weapons and beasts. All the vices, in human form, like anger, lust, arrogance and others were serving her. But the moment that army reached before Lord Kalki's forces they lost much of their lusture.

Lord Kalki was disturbed somewhat to find his forces losing their valour and enthusiasm. Immediately he reached before the enemy army and cast a glance toward Mayadevi, his own illusive power. All of sudden a ray of light emerged from her eyes to enter Lord Kalki's eyes. This made the Buddhist forces cry in great nervousness and panic. How could they would have fought against someone who was the master of their army's most powerful lieutenant? They started to wail aloud and felt almost powerless.

All the followers of Buddha were bewildered to find Maya-devi, as though vanishing in thin air. They had no idea that she was actually handmaiden of Lord Kalki, the tenth incarnation of Lord Vishnu. When, after absorbing the influence of Mayadevi, Lord Kalki looked at his own forces, they had regained their power and lustre as before. Now in order to destroy the Mlechcha forces totally, Lord Kalki took his renowned sword and rode on his favourite steed. He looked a picture of chivalry stationed on his horses with the sword in his hand and the bow on his back and the quiver fixed near his right shoulder. He had his golden armour having a large gun in the centre which gave the impression as though the Pole-Star was shining with its pristine glory. He, whose one glance is enough to captivate the most resolute woman, glanced at the army forces. His this form made his devotees enthralled in ecstasy. But he appeared truly deadly to the followers of the Buddha who began to shiver in dread. This way the same form of God appeared differently to the enemies and the followers, depending very much upon the intention they looked at Lord Kalki.

Beholding Lord Kalki getting victorious, all the gods stationed in the sky and beholding the spectacle below said: "Now the Yagya-altar—(battle field) – would have again the offering of Agni. Lord Kalki is the protector of the noble and holy, the destroyer of the infidels, the destroyer of his devotees' foes. He is the sustainer of all beings. May such Lord Kalki ever ensure our welfare in every way."

3
Preparation For Taking On The Kali Forces

Sootaji told the sages assembled at the holy spot of Nemisharanya that as Lord Hari came into the battle field again, that devotees' protector pierced certain infidels[1] with his unerring keen arrows while some of them were hacked off to pieces by his electric sword. Following Lord Kalki, his camp followers like King Vishaakh Yoop, Kavi, Pragya, Sumantraka, Gargya, Bhargya, and Vishaala also sent myriads of the infidels to hell. Seeing the Kalki forces appearing unstoppable, from the enemy side came forward Kapotrama, Kakaksha, Kakakrishna, Shuddhodaka and other Buddhists to face Lord Kalki. Then ensued such a bloody battle that all beings were terrified. In utter distress they started hymning Lord Hari, the Ultimate Saviour. The whole battle field seemed covered with blood and flesh which made the lord of ghosts ecstatic in expectation. The surging stream of blood made the horses look like the boats floating on that stream. The human hair gave the impression as if grass was growing at banks. The wave of rising bows made that stream appear all the more deadly. The elephants looked like small bridges over that stream, the hacked off heads the floating tortoises, and the shorn hands like fishes. That stream reverberated with the howls and hissing of the jackals and falcons to give the impression of a sounding war bugle. In the battle field the elephant rider fought with an elephant rider, horse-rider with a horse-rider, camel-rider with camel-rider – in short the stalwarts fought with someone matching in status. Every second scores of hacked off hands and feet covered the ground. The forces of

---

1   The term is Mlechcha which literally means a barbarous person speaking alien language and eating beef.

Lord Kalki showered arrows with such frequency and peneration that no Mlechcha soldier was left unwounded.

Seeing their soldiers and warriors alike faring rather poorly at the battle field, their devoted wives thought of entering the arena, neglecting the care of their kids and family. Some of them reached the battle field riding an elephant, or a cart or even the huge birds or the beasts of burden. They were covered by various ornaments and armours. They had a variety of swords and other weapons in their hands. Some of them were extremely beautiful, some ugly; some devoted to their husbands while some were drunk in wine – but nearly all the womenfolk of the Mlechcha army gathered in the battle field to take on the forces of Lord Kalki.

They valiantly came forward to replace their wounded spouses. The forces of Lord Kalki were rather surprised to find the enemy-women so chivalrously taking on the Kalki Army. Some of the commanders of Lord Kalki Army rushed to the Lord to tell him about the Mlechcha women's audacity. Getting the message Lord Kalki immediately reached the battle-front flanked by his lieutenants and followers. Seeing the women so committed to fight, Lord Kalki accosted them: "O women! Before starting the hostilities, listen to some advice that I offer for your benefit. First of all you must realise that it is not meant for the women to take up cudgels against men-forces."

Hearing this piece of advice, nearly all the Mlechcha ladies began to laugh. They replied, "O Lord! We owe our existence to our husbands. The moment they lost, we were also deemed the loser. But we must have to observe our ordained duty, come what may." And saying so they began to hurl weapons on the Lord. However, their weapons couldn't reach their destination. Immediately, there appeared the presiding deities of the weapons. They said: "O women! The power that we grant to the weapons has its fount in this Lord who stands against you. It is the inspiration that we derive from him that makes us act the way we do. Realise that you all are up against Lord Supreme who rules over the three realms. It is by His grace that we make the weapons reach their target and damage the opponents. The whole Nature follows his dictates only as the entire world pulsates at his inkling only. Even the very consciousness of the mundane relationships emerge by his grace only. The Maya is, in fact, his handmaiden which creates all sorts of mundane relations. All affection and hatred, preferences and predilections take their root in all beings' ken when Lord Hari wills so."

"O Ladies! Remember that we are not weapons but mere instrument of His will only. A weapon is a dead object; it gets power to damage its target only when the thought behind the action wants its to act that way. That thought is controlled by the weapon-weilders' mind which in turn gets controlled by His will only."

Listening to this discourse given by their weapons' presiding deities, the Mlechcha women were amazed. Perhaps guided by their destiny, still they reached before the forces of Lord Kalki. Deeming them to be so committed to action, like Lord Krishna had done before the beginning of Mahabharat, Lord Kalki also enlightened them on "Gyan Yoga", Atmanishthatmaka Gyan Yoga (enlightenment of knowledge for the sake of self-realisation), 'Medashraya' (following the mundane duties), 'Nishakarmtvaka Lakshana' (the symptoms showing the action without the desire of any return) etc. Thus enlightened the ladies performed their duties and were granted salvation which is rare to obtain even for the high sages. Having cleared the feminine obstruction Lord Kalki performed the terrible deed of getting rid of the Buddhist and Mlechha forces. This tale even by mere listening ensures salvation to the bings.

Having recounted the story of Lord Kalki's getting rid of the forces, Soota ji told the high sages: "O sages, thus accomplishing a comprehensive victory over Mlechcha and Buddhist forces, Lord Kalki left for Keekatpuri and appropriated all the riches and wealth that the city could offer. After staying for some time he, then, left for Chakrateertha, a very holy spot where he had ceremonial bath with full ritual. Then he started dwelling there for some time with his kith and kin.

While he was staying there, one day he found some holy sages in a very pitiable condition, seeking shelter under his grace. They were extremely frightened and they all supplicated in a very pathetic tone before Lord Kalki: "O Lord of Universe, O sustainer of this world! Please save us!" Lord Kalki looked at them. They looked very miserable. They wore just torn clothes and had their bodies very weak and emaciated. Included among them were the famous Balkhilya Rishis. Lord Kalki said, "O sages, where have you come from? Please tell me in details as to what is the cause of your feeling so disturbed and frightened. Just tell me who is that person. Even though that may be Indra, I would destroy him."

Hearing such reassuring words, the sages felt somewhat relieved and told him about the tyrant daughter of the demon-lord Nikumbha. They said: "O Lord! You know well that Kumbhakarna had this son Nikumbha whose daughter – a massive person – is Kuthodari. She is as tall as to scrape the sky when she walks. She is married to the demon-lord Kaalkanja from whom she has a son called Vikanja. Now keeping her head on the Himalayas and feet on the mount Nishad, she is feeding her son. Even her exhaling and inhaling have let loose storms in our vicinity, to cause us great disturbance. Distressed by her we have sought your shelter. Now only you can provide us succour. Please protect us from that huge woman."

Getting the details about Kuthodari, Lord Kalki, who never lets his devotees suffer, took his whole army and left for the Himalayas. Reaching in the valley, Lord Kalki took rest during the night. In the morning as he started to move toward his destination, they all espied a huge river of milk flowing close by. The milk in the river was white and fair. But all were befuddled seeing that massive river of milk. Although Lord Kalki was aware about that river he pretended ignorance and asked the complaining sages as to what was that river's name: "How come it is full of milk?"

"O Lord", the sages said: "We wanted to tell you in detail about this very river of milk. It is being created by the milk oozed out from the massive breast of that gargantuan demoness Kuthodari. O Great Lord! After seven ghadis (about 10 hours) yet another river of milk will start flowing and this one will be dried." "It is really amazing," uttered the Lord: "Milk oozed out by a demoness' breasts is becoming such a mighty stream of the milky-river! She ought to be truly of astronomical size to have breasts oozing such huge amount of milk as to make a river of milk flow this way."

"She is really of incomparable size, O Lord," the sages said. Lord Kalki then started going toward that demoness. Soon they spotted that demoness feeding her child. Her exhalations were is forceful as to make even the elephants lose their foothold on the earth. His body was truly huge. Even her bristle holes were as big as to make the deers enter them and relax with their pups. She really looked like a huge hill herself. When the soldiers saw her they were visibly frightened. Seeing them so much afflicted with fright, Lord Kalki asked all his soldiers to stay put there itself. He took along only the elephant and horse riders. With a selected squad of the army soldiers he left to take on that huge demoness.

As he moved ahead he shot a volley of very keen arrows on that demoness, Kuthodari. She felt quite disturbed and her feeding her child was obstructed. In annoyance she let out a huge roar to pulverise all the surroundings. Now she opened her huge cave-like mouth. With huge force she started sucking in the chariots, horses and elephants that accompanied Lord Hari. So much so that entire region's all loose objects including the armed forces kept on being pushed into her mouth. While the holy men mediating there started cursing the demoness, she couldn't care less.

The gods also grew panicky. They started praying for Lord Hari. Lord Kalki, who was himself the incarnate form of Lord Hari, was also disturbed. He, then, began to concentrate on invoking his powers. But in the meanwhile she also sucked the Lord into her mouth, to the great chagrin of the gods. Lord Kalki realised that the time of reckoning had dawned. So he began to cast her Maya (illusive play) while inside the demoness's stomach. He created a raging fire inside her stomach and began to cast his sword's blows at her intestines. And the way Indra had come out piercing the stomach of Vritra, Lord Hari also came out of her stomach with his chosen elephants, soldiers and horses. Some of the other soldiers came out of the stomach through various other openings. As they emerged out they started to cast their massive blows with their weapons on to that demoness's body. Then Lord Kalki made a terrific blow on to the head of that demoness who died instantly with a massive shriek pulverising the whole universe. That demoness, eventually, was killed by Lord Kalki.

When Nikanja, the son of demoness Kuthodari, saw this end of his mother, maddened in rage, he entered the enemy ranks and began to physically beat the soldiers with his bare hands. That dreadful son had the garland of elephant heads round his neck. He had a horrendous crown of snakes on his head and rings of lions' nails on his fingers. Unable to see his mother's so sorry an end, he began to torture the soldiers of the forces of Lord Kalki. Although in age he was hardly five years old yet being Kuthodari's son he looked much big. He was much powerful to torture Lord Kalki's forces. When Lord Kalki found him to be too troublesome, he used his Brahmastra to hack off his head in a trice. Nikanja's head was cut off and it fell on to the ground.

This way Lord Kalki slayed Kuthodari and her son Nikanja to provide relief to the sages and holy men. They gratefully assembled round him to sing paens in his glory. The gods rained flowers and the Gandharvas began to sing gratulatory songs. All the celestial musicians gathered there to hymn the Lord feelingfully. Having satisfied all beings of the region Lord Kalki left for Haridwar.

Reaching the holy precincts of the sacred city, he, along with his forces took a dip in the holy waters of the river Ganga. He passed a peaceful night there with his entire entourage. When he got up next morning he found many seers, holy men and sages standing before him hand-bound in a supplicative gesture. In order to gratify them he decided to pass some time in the Pindaraka forest, almost on the periphery of Haridwar.

One day, after having his bath in the merit-awarding river Ganga, Lord Kalki was seated in his chamber when some holy seers reached there to have his holy Darshan. Lord Kalki lovingly welcomed them and after giving them exalted seat, washed their feet reverentially. Then he said: "O Great Sages! You all are as dazzling as the mid-day sun. I am delighted to have you all close to me. Indeed, blessed is my life that such great sages have come to meet me."

Included among the sages were Vaamdeva, Atri, Vashishtha, Galava, Bhrigu, Parashara, Narada, Ashwathama, Kripacharya, Trita, Durvasa, Deval, Kauva, Ved Pramiti, Angira as well as two senior rulers of ancient times, Manu and Devapi. When Lord Kalki sought the introduction of the kings, King Manu said: "O Lord! The whole world is so well known to you—like the back of your hand. Even then if you want to know about my introduction, I give it. "O Lord! Brahma, the creator who had emerged from the lotus-flower shooting out from your naval, had a son called Maarichi whose son was Manu. Manu's sons were Satya Vikram and Ikshavaaku. Ikshavaaku's son was Yuvanashva → Mandhata → Puru-utsa → Anaranya → Trayadesya → Hariashwa → Aruna → Trishanku who had the renowned veridicious son Harish

Chandra. This truthful scion had Rohitashwa → Manu → Vrigu → Sagar. King Sagar had two queens who bore 100 and one son respectively. All of these perished because they tried to cheat sage Kapil. The one son's name was Asmanjas whose son was Anshuman. Seeing the sorry end of his grand uncles he requested sage Kapil to suggest something so that his perished grand uncles could have their merits duly rewarded. Kapil said: "For that you must bring down the celestial river Ganga on to the mortal plane. Although Anshuman's son Dileep did a lot for Ganga's descent to the earth, they couldn't succeed. Ultimately, it was Bhagirath who succeeded in bringing down Ganga on to the earth from heaven. Ganga's glory is undecayable and being the trickle that issued from Lord Hari's toe-nail, it shall remain here till Lord Hari is worshipped here."

"Bhagirath's son was Nabha. Then the lineage continued this way: Nabha → Sindhu Dweep → Ayutayu → Rituparna → Sudas → Saudasa → Madhavi → Ashmaka → Moolaka → Dashrath → Vishwasaha → Khatvaanga → Deerghabahu → Raghu → Aja → Dashrath (II). Lord Ram was the son of this Dashrath."

Hearing Lord Ram's name Lord Kalki wanted to know details about this incarnation (the 7th incarnation of Lord Vishu) although he knew about him well. But in order to show his curiosity he asked this question. King Manu was supremely delighted to get an opportunity to recount the tale of his most glorious forefather. Yet he said: "O Lord! even Sharada and the thousand-hooded Lord Shesha cannot cover Lord Ram's glories but I will try." Then he started recounting Lord Ram's tale.

In order to rid the world of demons and demoniac tendencies Lord Vishnu incarnated as Ram, the eldest son of King Dashrath from his seniormost queen Kaushalya. Darshrath had three more sons. Bharat, from Kaikeyi, Lakshman and Shatrughna from Sumitra. All the four were trained and educated by sage Vashishtha, the chief priest of the Solar Dynasty. Later on sage Vishwamitra took Ram and Lakshman along, to his hermitage which was being disturbed by the demons Khara Dushana, Tadaka – the demoness, Mareecha etc. Lord Ram with the assistance of his brave brother Lakshmana quelled the disturbance by either killing the demons or forcing them to flee to far off places. This way, right since his very tender age Ram had shown the signs of being some great incarnation.

Then both Ram and Lakshman, on Vishwamitra's advice, visited Mithila Nagari to attend the Swayamvara of King Janak's daughter, Sita. Although there had assembled many mighty kings and princes, it was Ram alone who won Sita in marriage by breaking the Bow of Shiv – the sole condition for winning Sita's hand in marriage. Ram was ceremonially married to Sita, while Bharat to Mandavi, Lakshman to Urmila and Shatrughana to Shrutikirti. These girls were the daughters of Janak's brothers. When King Dashrath was returning to Ayodhya with his sons, their wives and his entourage he met Lord Parashuram, a warrior sage, who appeared very wroth on them for Ram's breaking the bow of the sage's guru, Lord Shiv. However, Ram managed to satisfy the enraged sage.

As they reached Ayodhya, King Dashrath decided to appoint Ram as the king as he had grown old. But his queen Kaikeyi disturbed the proceedings by reminding the king about the two boons that he had promised to her. She, now, demanded throne to her son Bharat and banishment of Ram to jungles. Dashrath was greatly perturbed. He couldn't have gone back on his word to her but at the same time he never wanted his son Ram exiled. Ram heard about it and voluntarily offered to go in exile and leaving the throne for Bharat. As this happened, the king couldn't bear the shock of separation from his most beloved son, Ram, and expired. By this time Ram with Sita and Lakshman had gone to the forest. When Bharat, who had been, all this while, at his maternal father's place in Kaikaya Pradesh, returned. He severely condemned his mother Kaikeyi for her short-sightedness and selfishness. He decided to go to Chitrakoot where Ram had reached by then, and requested him to return to Ayodhya. But Ram declined for he had to honour his father's word. Eventually Bharat requested Ram to give his sandals which he made Ram's symbol to run the state affairs till the period of exile of Ram expired. Bharat returned to Ayodhya and Ram left for the jungles, further down south, with his brother Lakshman and wife Sita.

While Ram was in Dandakavana, in his leaf-made hut, a demoness, Shoorpnakha, the sister of the ruler of Lanka, Ravan, the demon-lord, tried to seduce the Ayodhya princes. Ram declined the offer and when she tried to seduce Lakshman, the latter hacked off her nose. Thus insulted, enraged Soorpanakha, left for Lanka to request her brother to take revenge for her insult. She also described Sita's beauty in superlative terms to tempt Ravan for abducting her. Ravan was hooked. He forced his associate Mareecha to masquerade as the golden deer in order to take Ram away from Sita. Mareecha performed the role so well that eventually Sita was left alone and Ravan abducted her. Ram was distressed. While moving in the jungles with Lakshman he happened to meet Hanuman, the lieutenant of the Monkey Lord Sugriva, who made Ram befriend Sugriva. Ram promised to make Sugriva king of the monkeys by removing Bali, the tyrant brother of Sugriva. This was achieved and Angad, the son of Bali, was made Surgiva's heir apparent. Now the search for Sita was undertaken under Sugriva's order. Hanuman led the search and managed to find Sita kept as captive in Ravan's Ashok Vaatika in Sri Lanka. At last, Ram, crossing the sea, managed to reach Lanka and slayed Ravan with the help of Ravan's son Vibhishan, to rescue Sita. After having purified Sita through the fire-test, Ram returned safely to Ayodhya with Sita and Lakshman. Bharat readily accepted Ram as the king and the latter was coronated. However, the trouble started again when a washerman condemned his wife for staying for a night at a stranger's place and adding: "I am not Ram to forgive your this act. He could pardon Sita but I can't pardon you. I reject you." Conditions developed in such a way that Ram had to desert Sita who was already pregnant. Sita was supported by the renowned sage Valmiki under whose protection she gave birth to her two sons – Luv and Kush. These kids defeated Ram's forces and when Ram came to fight against his own sons unknowingly, Sita, who knew the reality, could not bear this confrontation and sought refuge from Mother Earth. The earth parted and Sita entered the crevice. Ram returned with his two sons back to Ayodhya. After some time bequeathing the rule of Ayodhya to his and his brothers' sons evenly, Ram also left back for Vaikuntha, the eternal abode of Lord Vishnu."

Concluding the story Raja Manu said: "The lineage from Ram in which I was born started this way: Kush → Atithi → Nishadh → Nabh → Pundareeka → Kshemdhanva → Devaneeka→ Heen → Panipatra → Balakha → Ark → Rajabhama → Ranagana→ Vidhruta → Hiranyanabh → Pushpa → Dhruva → Syandava→ Agnivarna → Sheegra. Sheegra, a very valorous man, was my father. Some call me Budha and some Sumitra. Thus far I was engaged in a deep penance in a village called Kalapa. It was from Sage Vyas, the son of Satyavati, that I heard about your (Lord Kalki's) advent. Thus having waited for more than a lakh years after Kaliyuga's beginning, I now stand before you. I came here to seek your blessings and have your Darshan which is supposed to grant prosperity, happiness and peace to the aspirant."

Hearing about Manu's dynasty and getting his introduction, Lord Kalki said: "I have known that you were born in the Solar Dynasty of Lord Ram – a great family. I am delighted to have you before me. But who is the other noble man with you? I want to know about him as well."

Then Devapi started giving his introduction and telling about his lineage. "O Lord! Brahma, the creator, who emerged from the lotus growing out of your (Lord Vishnu's) navel, had a son called Atri. The synasty developed this way: Atri → Chandrama → Budh → Pururva → Nahush → Yayati → Yadu (from Devayani's womb) and Turvasu. Yayati's another wife Sharmishtha bore three sons: Drashyu, Anu and Puru. The way, in the beginning of the creation, five basic elements came in form, the same way Yayati's five sons came into being. Then the lineage continued this way: Puru → Janmejay → Prachinvan → Praveer → Manushyu → Abhayada → Uroo → Trayaruni → Pushkararooni → Vrihatkshetra → Hasti. It was this ruler Hasti who established the famous city Hastinapur." Then he gave the following details:

Hasti's sons were Ajameedha, Ahimeedha and Purumeedha. The lineage from Ajameedha started this way: Ajameedha → Riksha → Samvaran → Kuru → Pareekshit → Sudhama → Jahnu → Nishadha. Sudhamu's son was Suhotra and Suhotra's son was Chyavan. Then the lineage from Chyavan continued the following way: Chyavan → Vrihadrath → Kushagra → Rishabha → Satyajit → Pushpavana → Nahush. Vrihadrath's second wife gave birth to Jarasandha – the scounge of his enemies. Jarasandha's son was Sahdeva from whom the lineage continued the following way – Somaapi → Shrutashrva → Suratha → Vidoorath → Sarvabhaum → Jaisain → Rathaneeka. Rathaneeka's son was Yutayu, renowned for his fiery temperament. From Yutayu came Devatithi → Riksha → Dilip → Prateepak." While countnuing his narration to reveal the details of his lineage, Devapi told Lord Kalki: "I am Prateepak's son Devapi. After appointing my son, Shantanu, as the ruler

I started devoting my life exclusively in penance and worship in a remote village called Kalap. I have come here in order to have your Darshan. I have now also reverenced your feet in the company of other high sages and Manu." Lord Kalki was happy to get introduction of the two ex-kings and many other high sages as well as knowing their heart-felt feelings and he said: "Although I had sensed you to be the kings with supreme wisdom, now you both must adhere to my bidding and go back to your kingdoms to observe your royal duties truthfully."

Further he said that now after slaying the beastly, infidel Mlechcha I shall be coming to you (Manu) to appoint you as King of Ayodhya. And O royal sage, O Devapi, after killing Pukkar I shall have your ceremonial coronation performed at Hastinapur. I shall stay in Mathura and take care of your possible fears. I shall reestablish the rule of Satyuga after slaying the mighty demons like Shaiyyakarana, Ushtramukha and Ekajangha. Now you must also get rid of your ascetic appearance and don the royal robes and go back riding on your chariots. You both have enough mastery over martial weapons; you are mighty and intelligent. You may ever remain with me then."

Accosting Manu, Lord Kalki said: "King Vishaakh Yoop will solemnise his virtuous daughter's marriage with you. Hence you must act for public welfare obeying my instructions." Then you shall surely accomplish your objectives." Addressing King Devapi again, Lord Kalki said: "You must marry Ruchirashwa's daughter Shanta." Devapi, hearing Lord Kalki's instructions, was amazed and he thought in his mind: "No doubt whatever now remains in the assertion that Lord Kalki is in reality Lord Almighty (Vishnu)." While Lord Kalki was saying so, there appeared two beautiful chariots well bedecked with gems and full of divine weapons. Those chariots, wrought by Vishwakarma, created a ripple of curiosity even amongst those sages and rulers that were present there.

The Lord Kalki said: "This is a common knowledge that you two were born in noble dynasties for sustaining and protecting this world. You have come in form from the spark taken from the Sun, Moon, Yama and Kubera's personalities. Thus far you had kept your image hidden. Now since you have come to me, follow my instructions and get in these chariots sent by Indra himself." At Kalki's words the deities showered flower on the Lord while the high sages religiously hymned him. While the cool breeze was blowing, all of a sudden there appeared a very brilliant noble person. His mere presence was reassuring to the continuance of the righteous order undisturbed, and, at the same time, evaporating the mist of sins. Lord Kalki very reverentially welcomed him and asked in a meek tone: "Who your exalted self are? Blessed is our existence to have you in our midst. We are delighted to see sins perishing rather automatically."

Then, that brilliant person replied: "O Great Lord, I am Satyayuga, your ardent follower. I have come here tangibly for only having your Darshan. You are Supreme and Timeless Time. The whole universe but an illusion (Maya) wrought by you. It is your authority which governs all seasons, movements time and all Manus."

That Brahmachari again said: "First Manu was Swayambhoo, then Swarochish → Uttama → Tamas → Raivat → Chaakshasu, Vaivaswat → Sovarnika → Daksha Savarni → Brahma Savarni → Dharma Savarni → Rudra Savarni → Veda Savarni and the 14th was Indra Savarni. This 14th Manu is your replicate glory. They all come to rule with your inkling. Now, 12000 divine years make a cycle of the four Yugas (Ages). Out of this 4000 divine years measure a Satyayuga, 3000 Treta, 2000 Dwapar and 1000 years Kali Yuga. Each of these ages has the transitional period of respectively 400, 200 and 100 years. The remaining years also pass in the same order[1]."

"Every Manu rules for 71 Chaturyugis (four Ages' Cycles). This way their order follows. Brahma's One Day is equal to 14th Manu's entire reign. His night is also of even duration. This way the whole system of time and period continues. When Brahma completes his 100 years of ages, he dissolves himself. Then follows the emergence of the Primal Man (Lord Vishnu) from whose navel emerges a fresh creator. I am Satya Yuga personified form of that time cycle. During my tenure righteous order is religiously followed. Since every moral dictate is followed with total propriety, the scholars

---

1. According to other mythological texts the divine 12000 years are divided the following way. Satya 4800, Treta 3600, Dwapar 2400, Kali Yug 1200 which appear mathematically more logical.

also call me Krita Yuga." Getting this introduction from Satya Yuga Kalkiji was immensely pleased. Having seen Satya Yuga casting his shadows, Kalki, who had incarnated for the sake of ending the Kali Yuga, expressed his desire of taking on this Age at Virasan City. He started instructing his followers, capable of fighting, astride the elephants and horses – as also the pedestrian forces – to follow him to the battle field. He asked his lieutenant to sift such soldiers from the lot and make them ready. Thus Satya Yuga advanced, inspired Lord Kalki to fight decisively against Kali Yuga and do it in finally.

Sootaji told the sages in the holy place of Nemisharanya that obeying Kalkiji's order Manu and Devapi got married and riding their superior chariots came there to assist Kalkiji. Both the kings had developed arrogance on account of their valour and chivalry. They had illimitable forces and they were wearing impenetrable armours. Their forces, nearly six Akshohini, were trembling the earth with their movement. Vishaakh Yoop had also joined Lord Kalki's expedition with his one lakh elephants, one crore horses and two lakh pedestrian forces. The breeze was blowing and fluttering the soldiers' headgears' edges. Apart from them, there were distinct, red hued 50,000 horses, 10,000 elephants, many super stalwarts and nine lakh pedestrian troops.

Situated at the centre of this huge collection of the war-happy forces was Lord Kalkiji – as if Indra stood there flanked by his million strong divine forces. At the appointed auspicious time Lord Kalki started his expedition. Suddenly they confronted a Brahmana, who was Dharma personified, sent by Kali Yug. He was acompanied by Rita Prasad Abbaya, Sukh, Prasannata, Roga, Artha, Adanpa, Summati, Kshema, and Pratishnaya like assistants[1]. Thus Dharma reached there with all his attributes in order to have holy Darshan of Lord Kalki.

Seeing the holy Brahmana (Dharma) reaching there all of a sudden, Lord Kalki duly welcomed him and sought his introduction: "O Brahmana! Please enlighten me as to who you are and where are you coming from. Physically you

---

1. All these are symbolic representations of truth, happiness, pleasure etc.

appear rather run down but like a holy noble man you have come here with all your assistants, progeny and spouse. Which kingdom have you come from and for what purpose? Please tell me all the details about you?"

"I am born from your bosom, O Lord," said Dharma. "My norms set the norms of propriety of this world. Under your instruction I keep visiting all the places in order to help the noble and honest people. At present Shaka, Kamboja and Shabar etc. rule in Kali Yuga. Time has made me accept defeat from Kali Yuga. O Lord of the Entire Cosmos, this is the time when all the noble and holy sages and people are getting troubled and tortured. So I have come to seek shelter in your shadow. Please rid me and the earth of Kali Yuga's iniquities."

"Be not afraid, O Dharma," said Kalki reassuringly. "Now Satya Yuga has started casting his shadows. I am also supported by these noble kings like Manu and Devapi who assumed form under Brahma's guidance to enhance your influence. At Keetaka City I have already trounced the Buddhist forces which never believed in God. I am also planning to get rid of those who are not followers of Vishnu and who also defy your norms. My forces are ready to depart. Hence there is no reason why you should feel scared. I assure you to roam about the earth fearlessly as I am (my forces) ever with you." Further assuring Dharma, Lord Kalki said: "Now Satya Yuga is also casting its shadows and I am also here. So you must stop worrying and move about the world without fear."

Thus reassured Dharma felt rejuvenated. Mentally reverencing him he started to leave the place with his entire team. He left his spouse at the hermitage of a perfect sage. He then adopted the appearance of an ascetic. At that moment the Vedas appeared before him in the form of a chariot and the various holy scriptures came before him adopting the form of various weapons like bows and arrows. The seven main notes became the seven horses drawing the Veda-Chariot, the Brahmana (Dharma) acted as the charioteer. With this paraphernalia Lord Kalki also departed on his victory expedition. Dharma also felt quite strengthened, having been reassured by Lord Kalkiji. With victory as their target they left to take on Kali Yuga.

The army of Kalki soon reached the abode where Kali Yuga lived. The place was haunted and dogs were barking all around. The crows were crowing and the owls were letting out eerie noises. When Kali Yuga learnt about Lord Kalki's arrival, readying his chariot marked with an owl sign, and accompanied by his progeny, he set out to meet him. Soon a huge herd of the dark forces emerged out of that Vishanampuri. Seeing the enemy before them, Lord Kalki ordered his lieutenant to start the assault. And chanting the holy words of the Vedas, so auspicious to start a noble endeavour, Lord Kalki's army took on the evil forces of the Kali Age.

4

The Decisive War

As the battle commenced Dambha began to fight with Ritu and Lobha against Prasad. Krodha took on Abhaya while Sukh began to take up cudgels against Bhaya. Nivaya made a terrible ouslaught on Preeti. Aadhi took on Yoga, Vyadhi on Kshema, Glani on Prashraya and Jara with Summati. Since the starlwarts were of matching strength a terrible war ensued there. Brahma and all other deities assembled in the sky to watch the hair-raising terrible war with great delight as they knew that the evil forces had their days numbered. Extremely valorous Rabash and the Kambojas took on Manu. Devapi engaged himself in a duel against Chauma and the barbaric forces. Vishaakh Yoop Naresh took on Pulinda and other lowly caste people. Meanwhile Sri Bhagawan Kalki started his battle against Koka and Vikoka. The last two warriors had become very arrogant as they had received a boon from Brahma. The two brothers looked identical and their unified strength always pulverised even the gods. They possessed very great strength and were overtly ambitious to rule over the entire earth. Seeing them fighting in a terrible mood, Dharma thought of repulsing their penetrating force. He came before them. Kali tried to jointly face Dharma and Satya (Yuga) but panicked and fled on his mount, an ass. His chariot having an owl emblem fluttering on his flag was broken to pieces. When Kali entered his citadel, he was a wounded person with blood trickling down his wounds. His blood's pungent odour was filling the entire atmosphere. This way while Kali escaped to save himself, his other lieutenants also fared no better. Krodha stood defeated against Abhaya. Bhaya had to breathe his last when attacked by Sukha. Preeti's powerful fisty blow made Nigya die helplessly. Satya Yuga's arrow showers made Aadhi –Vyadhi run away in utter panic.

Having defeated the opponents Satya Yuga entered the capital city, Vishasha. Seeing them coming Kali tried to run away, but since his all body parts had been burnt and his wife and progeny almost dead, weeping bitterly Kali quietly entered his unmanifest years. Meanwhile, employing his deadly weapons Raja Manu destroyed Kambojas. Raja Devapi also destroyed Chola and Barbar (barbaric) race. While all this transpired, mighty Vishaakh Yoop also destroyed powerful Pulinda and Pukhasa warriors. This way, by grace of Lord Kalki, Dharma and Satya Yuga successfully achieved the destruction of their foes.

However, Koka-Vikoka still fought defiantly and bravely. They were grandsons of Shakuni and son of Vakasura. Eventually, like Vishnuji had destroyed Madhu-Kaitabha, the same way Lord Kalki slayed both the brothers with an unerring javelin (spears) attack. However, these demoniac scions were well versed in black magic. They knew how to revive the dead. No matter how many times Lord Kalki slayed them their hacked off head repeatedly combined with the trunk to bring them back to life. Even when their bodies were shredded to pieces they again revived themselves – this time holding the tail of Lord Kalki's horse. So miserably the two brothers, Koka and Vikoka, were holding the tail of Lord Kalki's horse as though a distressed child holds on to his mother's hand. Even though the demon duo were distressed, they had not yet accepted their defeat.

However, Lord Kalki's horse felt annoyed when its tail was pulled by the demon duo and using its hind legs it cast a deadly blow at the breast of the demon duo. They fell on to the earth, losing their conciousness. But soon they recovered and beholding Lord Kalki again before them, they began to cast their blows. The demon duo began to wage battle with renewed strength. Seeing the battle prolonging endlessly, Lord Brahma, the creator, appeared there to advise Lord Kalki: "O Lord! These two demons are very powerful as being blessed with a boon of immortabity. They can be killed only when they are attacked in such a way that during the attack they shouldn't be able to behold each other. Hence they are to be killed in one blow and simultaneously. Just place yourself between them and cast a fatal fisty blow on each demon's temple simultaneously."

Lord Kalki did exactly the same. He immediately placed himself amidst the demon duo without any weapon in his hand. Then making a fist of his fingers he used both the hands to cast a deadly blow on each demon's temple. The intensity of the blow reduced their heads to smithereens. This way only those deadly demons could be destroyed by Lord Kalki. With their heads smashed they fell on to the ground the same way as the mountains collapse when their peaks are smashed away.

As the two demons were done in, the celestial musicians, Gandharvas and Kinnar began to sing in relief and ecstasy. All the noble saints and seers were delighted. The moment Koka, Vikoka were slain Kavi, the commander of Kalki, was charged enough to kill ten thousand stalwarts of the opponents. Meanwhile Praagya killed a million soldiers of the Mlechchas. Lord Kalki began to launch the expedition on Shaiyyakarma demons. As he moved ahead he was followed by hundred of soldiers.

Continuing the story Soota ji said that after slaying these demons called Koka-Vikoka, Lord Kalki rode upon his horse and led his victorious army to the City of Bhallat. But the ruler of this kingdom deemed him to be direct incarnation of Lord Supreme, Vishnu, and in panic he abandoned the city. At that time Lord Krishna's devotee, supremely radiant, Raja Shashidhwaja was besides himself with great joy. His wife Sushanta always observed the fasts to please Lord Vishnu with great religiosity. She was also devoted to her husband. When she beheld her husband going out to wage a battle against Lord (Kalki) Vishnu, she said, "O Lord, O Master! The one you intend facing is none else but Lord Supreme Vishnu. How would you be able to cast your blows on him? How can you fight against your chosen lord?"

Explaining the norms of propriety, Shashidhwaja told her: "Sushanta, dear ! Do not be afraid. You know that Lord Brahma has set certain norms of propriety – according to them one cannot refuse to fight should one be challenged by his own Guru, disciple or even one's chosen Lord himself. In such conditions facing the challenge squarely is entirely proper. Hence I must go to fight as my chosen Lord himself has challenged to take up cudgels against him." Thus explaining Raja Shashidhwaja left for the battle field to take on Lord Kalki.

While he was departing, Sushanta accosted him: "One enjoys one's kingdom's pleasure only when one returns safe and sound from the battle field. Even if one gets killed in the battle observing one's duty one goes to heaven after death. This way for a true Kshatriya either situation offers rich reward. But the question is: "Would you be able to hurl weapons on your chosen god, Lord Hari?"

Then Shashidhwaja again elaborated on his ideal course of action. "If one does one's duty without desiring any reward, one gets no stigma on his name. This is what Lord Krishna – the 8th Incarnation of Lord Vishnu—had explained in his famous discourse called Gita. There are certain duties that one does due to one's having the body assigned to a particular community. Sincerity is the hallmark of the true relationship between the Lord and the disciple. It is following the same ideal that I am going to fight the battle against my chosen Lord." Sushanta was delighted to get such wise words uttered by her husband. She lovingly touched his feet and the king embraced her feelingfully. Then keeping his mind fixed on Lord Hari, he left for the battle field. Shashidhwaja deemed himself to be singularly fortunate to face his chosen Lord in the battle field.

Soon a fierce battle commenced. The royal heir Suryaketu took on Raja Manu. Suryaketu's younger brother Vrihatketu was very soft-limbed person but quite deft in the mace duel. He started fighting with Raja Devapi. Meanwhile, Raja Vishaakh Yoop came astride on an elephant to fight against Shashidhwaja. Shashidhwaja was riding a red horse. He was also accosted by the famous archer Bhargya. This way the entire battle field was covered by a variety of weapons that were being traded on each other by the warriors. All were showing their valour. Due to the fierce fighting taking place and the dust raised by the vehicles and persons' movement, darkness had enveloped the battle field.

The gods had assembled in the heavens to watch the tumultuous battle being fought there. All the Gandharvas and other demi-gods had also assembled there. The blowing of the conches and the battle drums were creating deafening sound. The sound was so piercing and intensive that many warriors had become rather stunned by the impact. The war was enhancing the work load of the Yama-loka. Eventually the opponents of Lord Kalki's forces lost their will to fight. They began to scatter away in panic. Thousands of soldiers had lost their life. Many breathed their last getting trampled under foot. Many were asphyxiated and some were lynched to death. There were thousands who had lost their limbs.

While narrating the story Sootaji told the seers that the battle consumed the life of thousands. A massive stream of blood had started flowing amidst the battle field. The flowing headgears of the soldiers in that stream gave the impression as though swans were floating. The elephants lying there booked like small island emerging out of that field's stream. The shorn limbs of the soldiers appeared as though fish were making merry rounds in that eerie stream. Suryaketu had a terrible fight against King Manu. Both fought very bravely but soon they fell severely wounded. When King Manu's charioteer saw his master's that alarming condition he drove him to safety. Meanwhile, mighty Vritaketu showered a volley of keen arrows upon Raja Devapi. He looked totally covered with the arrows. But soon Raja Devapi gathered courage, took his ten keen arrows to start his retaliatory attack. Seeing his brother's serious condition, Vrihatketu came to his rescue. He cast a powerful fisty blow upon Raja Devapi and made him fall unconscious. Then he started to slaughter king Devapi's army.

Meanwhile, Raja Shashidhwaja saw Lord Kalki exactly before him. Seeing him he was reminded of his chosen Lord, Krishna. Brilliant as the sun in mid-heaven, covered in his Pitambar (Yellow raiment), adorning the fragrance bestowing shining diadem, long armed, radiating light from his resplendent face – Lord Kalki appeared true replica of Lord Krishna. If any soldier dared to gaze at him, his eyes were blinded with the dazzling light. Lord Kalki was flanked with many noble kings like Raja Vishaakh Yoop, Satya and Dharma who were rendering him constant service with full devotion.

Beholding that image of Lord Kalki, Raja Shashidhwaja was besides himself with great joy and delight, for he thought as though he was beholding his chosen Lord Krishna. Possessed by the emotional ecstasy he burst into his improvised prayer: "O Lord with blue lotus like eyes, I hymn you. Please come and attack at my heart. In order to save yourself from the volley of my keen arrows it is better you hide yourself into my heart. He who is formless yet gets manifest, who is desireless but acts without any desire of return, who has no enemy but capable of slaying thousands of my soldiers! It is my good great fortune that I face him in the battle field. O Lord! I shall be hitting you with my keen arrows. Nevertheless, even then if I deem you different than your Supreme Spirit Form, I should be consigned to that realm wherein go those that visualise the difference between the images of Lord Shiv and Lord Vishnu. May I suffer the same consequences if I distinguish between your that conceived image and the present image."

Hearing Raja Shashidhwaja uttering these words, though internally he was pleased but externally he pretended extreme anger. In that fit of rage Lord Kalki started hurling weapons at Raja Shashidhwaja. The king also retaliated but his all arrows were cut half-way. Raja Shashidhwaja was amazed to see such ineffectiveness of his arrows. He was naturally charged to thrust in a volley of arrows around Lord Kalki's chariot. These arrows did hurt Lord Kalki who was cut to the quick to take revenge. Now ensued a fierce war between the devotee and the God. They both resorted to using the divine weapons like Brahmastra, Parvatastra, Aagneyaastra etc. They also hurled the counterweapons to nullify these astras. All the dwellers of the earth and heaven were pulverised into petrification seeing a fierce war taking place before them. They were as much afraid to apprehend as though the Deluge was round the cover. The fire let out by these divine weapons were really scorching. But seeing the divine weapon getting nullified, Raja Shashidhwaja decided to enter the close duel with the Lord. With this intention he kept aside his missiles and entered the fray with sword and other similar weapons. Then ensued the duel in which both the expert warriors used their hands and feet quite deftly. Since both had sturdy physique they fought very bravely and cunningly.

All of sudden Lord Kalki let out a fierce roar exactly like Lord Vishnu in his Boar Incarnation had uttered after redeeming the earth to its normal position. It was accompanied by a swift head-below to Raja Shashidhwaja. The blow made Raja Shashidhwaja visibly disturbed. But brave as he was, he got out of that painful swoon and stood up once again. Then he made a fisty blow on the body of Lord Kalki. This was too powerful a blow and even Lord Kalki lost his consciousness. Seeing this Dharma and Satya (Yuga) grew panicky and began to take him out of the battle field. But Raja Shashidhwaja made their plan a blatant failure. So much so that Raja Shashidhwaja pressed both Dharma and Satya into his armpit with his hands, making them ineffective. Then he carried the unconscious Lord Kalki to his palace with due reverence.

Reaching home, Raja Shashidhwaja grew rather complacent that "let alone me, even my sons cannot be trounced by Indra. Now Lord Kalki is under my control and his entire army stands defeated."

When Raja Shashidhwaja reached home he found his wife Sushanta in the temple of Vishnu surrounded by many Vaishnava devotees. All were lost in the worship. Seeing this devotional spectacle Raja Shashidhwaja said to his wife: "Dear Sushanta! You will feel delighted to know that the self-same Lord Vishnu, who in response to the prayer of the gods had condescended to appear as Kalki Incarnation in the village Sambhal in the house of the Brahmana called Vishnu Yasha, who had destroyed all the Mlechcha and alien powers, is now very much in our house. Under the pretension of his becoming unconscious, he has been brought here. But he is here to test the depth of our devotion. O beloved! You must be seeing that Dharma and Satya have also come here, being pressed in my arm-pits. So while you worship the installed God, please also take care of these guests, who also represent the same god." Getting these details Sushanta was supremely delighted: "The self-same god, Lord Vishnu's Incarnation, has come to my house!" She was amazed but very respectfully she welcomed them and then forgetting all the worldly etiquettes started to sing and dance while moving around Lord Kalki! She began to sing devotional songs accompanied by her follow worshippers. Sushanta was so much lost in her feeling that she began to address Lord Kalki in the following way: "Victory to thee, O Lord! O Lord of the World, adorable by Indra, adorned with a beauteous raiment and ornaments, ever reverenced by holy saints, please make me adore these feet without any inhibition. Your grand form, the repository of all global riches, dweller in all the holy seers' heart is quite captivating. Hence, O Lord, please fulfil our all desires. Your praise-singing is capable of destroying all afflictions of the world. Your sweet voice emerging out of your beautiful countenance grants instant happiness to all. O Lord of all the gods, your glittering face's vision ensures welfare of all. O victor of all and vangquisher of the mightiest, should you deem my committing any felony in your estimation, please forgive me immediately. You are God and hence it is not meat for you to nurse any ill-will for any one. O Lord of the World! Be ever gracious to me."

"O Lord! The world sustains itself because of the five elements created by you. With your three quality creations you show your effect all over the world. O Lord! 'Kirtan' of your glories ensures destruction of all the afflictions of this Kali Age. When the beings of this world chant your holy name they even get redeemed from the vicious cycle of births and deaths." Sushanta further said: "O Lord Supreme, you always incarnate yourself in the world for strengthening the rule of propriety and for quelling the brewing iniquitious chaos. May your this incarnation prove beneficial to all of us! I wish you may keep my house full of pleasure, comfort and happiness. I know that without your grace nothing succeeds in this world – neither one gets real happiness nor one comes in real pleasure. O Lord! Please ensure my unwavering faith in your feet. Should you disallow we beings reverentially worshipping you, we might perish in a trice."

"O Lord! Astride your horse you roam about everywhere. Those who perish by your keen arrows get to your exalted realm only by your grace. Your visage's beauty pales into insignificance many full moons. Shiv and Brahma survive with your backing."

Totally gratified with Sushanta's these feelingful prayers, Lord Kalki stood up gracefully. He stood up the same way as a wounded soldier stands up as soon as he get consciousness. When Lord Kalki espied Sushanta in front, Satya Yuga on his left and Dharma on his right and Raja Shashidhwaja behind, he bent his head in shame and said: "O lotus eyed woman! O beautiful lady! Who are you? Why must you appear so much keen to render me any service? And how come this extremely valorous king Shashidhwaja is standing before me!" Then he asked Satya and Dharma as to how could be reach the private chamber of the adversary's palace. He insisted on being told in details as to how the ladies of the adversary were so delightedly willing to serve him. Moreover, he asked as to why was he not slain in the battle field by Raja Shashidhwaja when he (Lord Kalki) was so much wounded? Why had he brought him to the ladies chamber of his palace?

Then Queen Sushanta explained the reason to Lord Kalki: "O Lord! Who in this universe can overpower you? Who doesn't adore you – be him a demon, man or god? Lord! You are adorable in the entire world by all. In fact all the beings are your friends. Even your mere Darshan can remove any animus that one may be having for you. Had my husband been nursing animosity even in the least for you, he would not have escorted you to the safety of his own home. O mighty armed! Please rest assured as my husband is your servant and devotee and is ever prepared to gratify and please you. It is your name he stands by and chants unstoppably. This way even I am your hand-maiden. You are gracious, fount of all mercy and especially considerate to your devotees. Even though you may pretend whatever you want the fact is that you have come here only because you have a soft corner for us."

Hearing Sushanta's this feelingful explanation, Dharma said: "O Lord Kalki, the destroyer of all the affliction of the Kali Age, I feel supremely gratified listening to such an affectionate and feelingful welcome to you that is accorded by the royal pair here." Then Satya Yuga said: "Lord! I am feeling really blessed after having the Darshan of your true devotees. With their guileless devotion, your grace in the world has grown manifold." Raja Shashidhwaja couldn't help saying. "O Lord! Of late I seemed to have fallen prey to the temptations of Kama (lust), Krodha (anger) and other sensual attractions. Even when I know that you are Lord Supreme Personified, I had rebelled against my own soul to rain weapons upon your person. To tell you frankly, my soul was condemning my action." Whereupon in reply to Raja Shashidhwaja Lord

Kalki said with a smile: "O King! You have won me over in every way. I am extremely happy with your devotion and worship. Even Dharma and Satya (Yug) are fully gratified with your guileless devotion to me." Delighted at these tidings Raja Shashidhwaja recalled his both sons from the battle field and as advised by his queen, Sushanta, gladly offered his daughter Ramaa in marriage to Kalkiji.

On that auspicious occasion Raja Shashidhwaja invited all the kings and princes to attend the wedding. Kings like Manu and Devapi all assembled there to witness the holy marriage. In that marriage of Lord Kalki and Raja Shashidhwaja's daughter Ramaa, people of all caste and category had assembled with great gusto.

While narrating the details of that marriage, Sootaji told seers that after the marriage all the assembled kings and seers asked Raja Shachidhwaja as to what penances had the king observed in the past lives to get Lord Supreme as his son-in-law. How could be get such deep devotion to Lord Kalki? "Is it the outcome of an inborn urge he or has cultivated it through rigorous penance and prayers? O King! Please enlighten us as to what a being should do to get such unflinching worship to Lord Kalki."

On being asked this way, King Shashidhwaja told the inquisitive assembly after the marriage of Lord Kalki to his daughter Ramaa: "Many thousand years ago I was a vulture surviving on rotten meat. My wife Sushanta was a she-vulture. We both used to stay on a huge banyan tree in which we had carved a nest for us. We were able to move at will. Surviving on the rotten meat of the dead beings we were passing our life happily. One day an expert fowler happened to espy our nest. In order to catch hold of us he sent his pet vulture close to our nest. Since that fowler was ever staying close to us, we couldn't get much food for ourselves. Once getting sorely famished we came charging upon that tame vulture in order to eat its flesh. But that was the trap laid by that fowler in which we got ourselves entangled. The fowler was very pleased to find us trapped. He took us and dashed us against a rock on the bank of river Ganga. He did it so violently that we had our brains reduced to smithereens. But since that rock was a holy one, placed almost at the confluence of the river Ganga and Gandaki, we almost acquired Lord Vishnu's four-armed form and became radiant with our inherent glow. Riding up on an air-vehicle (Vimana) we were escorted to Lord Vishu's realm, Vaikuntha, where we lived for 100 Ages. Then we were shifted to Brahmaloka where we lived for 500 Ages. After having enjoyed the heavenly comfort for nearly 1000 Ages we were again sent to the mortal plane of the earth. We remember all these details because of the special quality of the waters of the river Gandaki. It is believed that those who expire in its waters remember their past lives' details forever. Moreover, that boulder against which we were dashed was of the family of the holy stone of 'Shaligram'. Since we had our constant contact with that holy stone, we could ascend to Vaikunth by virtue of that fact. But this knowledge also opened our inner-wisdom's eyes. We thought that if a mere contact with Lord Vishnu's favourite stone could take us to the realm of Vaikuntha, we may surely become inalienable part of Lord Supreme should we try to have unwavering devotion to that Great Lord. We had learnt from Brahmaji that the Lord will incarnate himself as Lord Kalki to end the afflictions of the Kali Age; we were sure to receive his grace and we have done exactly the same now."

Thus Shashidhwaja revealed the secret of his constant faith in Lord Hari and then donated 10,000 elephants, 1,00,000 horses, 6000 chariots, 600 young maidens, uncountable gems and jewel as dowry in marriage to Lord Hari. After this ceremony was over, the inquisitive kings further asked Raja Shashidhwaja: "How can one have such unshakable devotion to Lord – the Bhagwat Bhakti? What are the peculiarities of a Bhagwat Bhakta? What does he do, eat or speak? What are his mannerisms? O Lord of all the kings, you know all these details. Please enlighten us on these details for our immense benefit."

Raja Shashidhwaja was delighted to get this query from the kings. Then delving upon the doings of Lord Krishna he recited that tale which he had heard from the creator himself. Shashidhwaja said: "In the very beginning of the creation, all the great seers and sages were seated in the court of Brahma. At that time Narad had asked the same question which was replied by Sage Sanaka. I narrate you that conversation verbatim since I was also present in that ancient assembly.

When asked by Narad the child sage Sanak said: "He who keeps under control all his five senses is the real devotee. Having done so he must act in total conformity to his Guru's command. Because Guru is the 'Beacon' that takes the devotee to his destination – i.e. Lord Hari. The devotee under the Guru's guidance follows the path of devotion in all the nine ways as ordained by the Scriptures. Then he, as it were, acts only on behalf of his chosen Lord Hari. His no act is then ascribable to his own person. He carries no desire for any return but he establishes a direct but inseperable rapport with his chosen Lord."

The kings respectfully heard Raja Shashidhwaja and said: "O King! You are so well versed in scriptures and moral aspects of the highest order. How come you came to be associated with this war so full of violence? People like you are by nature non-violent." Whereupon Raja Shashidhwaja replied: "O Kings! One acts in accordance with one's inkling from destiny. May be this war was raged because I was destined to come closer to Lord Hari (Kalki). Moreover it is the Lord's sweet will that brought me to the battle field. In accordance with the Scriptural commandments, one should not shun from a war if it is thrust upon one no matter the challenger be one's chosen Lord Himself." Further dilating upon the norms of propriety Raja Shashidhwaja said: "Long ago, the authority on all Vedic knowledge, Sage Vedavyas had declared that letting go a crime unpunished is tentamount to being accomplice in the commitment of that crime. The same way those who don't act in accordance with the Vedic knowledge are held infidels. Such acts are not atoned by means of repentence as well. This way I acted in accordance with the Vedic instructions and fought the battle against even my chosen lord, Lord Kalki, Dharma and Satya. Even otherwise, I acted in the proper way. Lord Kalki (Vishnu) is the Master of universe and nothing happens against his will. He is the sole 'doer' of this universe. Even according to Vedas, killing in a fair battle cannot be equated with a slaughter. I acted in total accordance with His will. Hence my no action should activate any reaction, for I acted totally on his behalf and this way I incurred no sin."

Getting such pearls of wisdom from Raja Shashidhwaja all the kings present there were quite pleased. Then one of the kings asked him: "O Lord of the Land! According to scriptures Raja Nimi had to lose his body due to a curse he had received from Saga Vashishtha. But you seem to have grown totally indifferent to your body even after enjoying all the kingly affluence. How and why?"

Answering to their question, Raja Shashidhwaja said: "It is true that Raja Nimi had to lose his body due to sage Vashishtha's curse but it must be understood that one who lives in eternal communion with his chosen lord, the body is first a mere instrument for him. One has to be totally indifferent to self to realise this communion with self."

Narrating this highly enlightening incident, Sootaji told the sages, sitting before him totally lost in meditation, that following this narration, Raja Shashidhwaja requested Lord Kalki hand-bound that he might be permitted to go to Haridwar while his sons, grandsons and all other kings and princes would stay put there and that "O Lord Supreme, you are well aware of my intended purpose behind saying this. You are well aware about the slaughter that you had performed of the apes and bears like Jamavanta and Dvivida." While saying so the king started to depart in the company of his wife, Sushanta. But, all of a sudden, Lord Kalki bowed his head in shame. This made the kings present there wonder for the reason behind this gesture. Since curosity was uncontrollable, the kings asked Lord Kalki the reason behind his shameful gesture. But the Lord said: "I think the better person to ask this question is Raja Shashidhwaja himself. Perhaps he can answer your query best."

This made the kings ask Raja Shashidhwaja who was about to depart with his wife. When he was accosted by the kings be stayed put and said: "You remember in the olden age, when Ram's incarnation took place, Lakshman had slayed Ravan's son, Indrajit, and the demon was released from his demoniac form. But in doing so Lakshman had killed a Brahmana (since Ravan was of Brahmana family). With the result, the stigma of his slaying a Brahmana affected his body in the form of a fever. But one of the apes' lieutenents, Dwivid, the scion of the family of the physicians as renowned as the Ashvanikumaras, told him about a Mantra which had cured Lakshman of the afflictions. The text of the mantra was in a coded form which said: "SAMUDRA SYOTTARE TEERE DWIVIDO NAM VANARAH!" This was written in bold letters and hanged on a high point under Lord Ram's instructions. When Lakshman was totally cured of the stigma, he asked the ape, Dwivid, to have his boon as the reward. Dwivid was delighted and said: "O Lord! I desire death at your hand to get redemption from this ape-form." Whereupon Lakshman assured him that in the Dwapar Age when he would incarnate as Balram and he (Dwivid) as Soota putra Loma Harshna, the former would kill the latter in the holy place of Nemisharanya. And it happened exactly that way." Continuing the story, Raja Shashidhwaja told about Jamvant's also seeking a boon of similar genre. When in Vaman Incarnation Lord Vishnu sought the boon and received it from the demon lord, Raja Bali, Jamvant had worshipped his foot when it was placed in the top realm. Seeing Jamvant being so energetic and agile, Vaman asked the Bear to get his desired boon. Then also Jamvant asked his death by Lord Vishnu's Chakra Sudarshan so as to ensure his Moksha (liberation). Whereupon Lord Yama accepted to fulfil his desire in his incarnation as Lord Krishna in Dwapar age. Jamvant was redeemed during the episode of Syamantaka Mani which is a well known incident."

"I know all these details of Lord Kalki's earlier incarnations. I know well about his slaying Jamvant because I was born as Satrujit who laid a false charge at Lord Krishna for stealing the fabled gem. "I failed to get Moksha," confessed Raja Shashidhwaja, "because of that false charge. Now I have made good that shortcoming by my offering my daughter Ramaa (who is actually Satyabhama's incarnation) in marriage to the Lord. Also having known that killing by Sudarshana Chakra ensures one's Moksha, I also entertain this desire of getting killed by my own son-in-law (Lord Kalki) in the battle field. It is by recollecting his promise that Lord Kalki had bowed his eyes with shame." The king clarified the reason before the entire audience.

The assembly of the kings was touched by getting these noble details. Continuing the story Sootaji said: "When Raja Shashidhwaja ended his story, Kalkiji gratified the king with his soft words and left the place with the curious kings to get to his resting chamber. Raja Shashidhwaja after having received the desired boon left for Hardwar to worship Goddess Maheshwari.

×   ×   ×   ×

Meanwhile, Lord Kalki also entered the fortress covered with the steep mountain ranges. It was called Kanchanapura which was protected by the huge poisonous snakes. They would produce the streams of poison to protect the fortress. Lord Kalki fearlessly moved ahead to slay all the snakes to enter the gold treasure of the fort. This small city had huge deposits of gold protected by Naag Kanyas[1]. The city had good amount of the wish-fulfilling (Kalpa Vriksha) trees. But there were no human beings.

Beholding the unusual spectacle, Lord Kalki told the accompanying kings: "O kings! This city of serpents casts a mortal fear on humans. Hence they are nowhere to be found. Now you should all collectively decide whether we should enter this city or not." All were in a fix. That moment, all of a sudden a divine voice echoed from the skies:

"Don't enter the place accompanied by the kings. Because the moment the Vish-Kanyas look at them, they shall perish. You alone may enter it." Lord Kalki decided to follow the instructions and taking a dagger in his hand he alone entered it. As he moved in he espied a beautiful girl – a Vish-Kanya. She said to Lord Kalki: "O Lord! All the powerful kings and warriors of this realm have perished all of a sudden. I am extremely unhappy because I cannot be married to any demon, deity or man. But I am getting enamoured of your loveful sight, full of nectar of vision. I am a Vish-Kanya and I salute you. O Lord! I am dim-witted and rather unfortunate. O Lord! Tell me which penances or strict disciple I should observe to get to you." Kalkiji replied: "O comely waisted girl. First give me your detailed introduction and tell all about you. What has made you reach this stage? Is it due to any curse that you carry? What has made even your sight so venomous? What was your fault to make you get to this condemned stage?"

Getting this sympathetic treatment that Vish-Kanya said: "Great Lord! I am wife of the Gandharva, Chitragreeva, and my name is Sulochana. We both, husband and wife,

---

1. The typical youthful female reared up on snake's poison to kill any person on contact.

were merrily passing our life and my husband was fully satisfied with the pleasure that he derived from my body. Once we were thick in the amorous play on the rock of the mountain Gandhamadan and I was extremely charged. Drunk in the heady wine of my beauteous physique I was on cloud nine. There I also happened to behold a Yaksha-sage sitting on a rock. His body structure was asymmetrical. Seeing his physique I happened to pass a contemptuous remark. Although realising the sexual charge I was filled with, initially he tried to ignore me, I would not relent from my contemptuous saddism. At last, filled with anger he stood up. Taking handful of water from his Kamandal (water-pot) he cursed me: 'May your sight become venomous which is making me a butt of ridicule. Since then I am helplessly roaming about these toxic areas with no relief. Since my sight had become very toxic, the moment I gazed at my husband, he expired. Now I am here, moving shelterless and whiling my life in vain. I seem to have no way as my very sight showers poison on the viewed person and causes his or her death."

"I don't know which of my meritorious deed entitled me to have your Darshan in this deserted place. But I seem to have gained a nectareous sight and also feeling relieved from that curse. Now I want to go near my beloved husband. Moreover, this is also an amazing revelation to me that it is through this curse only that I could have your Darhsan and get absolved from that deadly curse."

Expressing her feeling this way and having felt greatly relieved, that Vish-Kanya, by the grace of Lord Kalki, got a divine aerial vehicle which eventually took it heavenwards.

After her departure Kalki Lord appointed Raja Mahamati as the ruler of that Puri. Raja Mahamati got a son called Amarsha in due time. The son was as brilliant as his father had been. Amarsha got a son named Sahastra who was full of discretionary wisdom. Sahastra's son became famous as Raja Asi. It is believed that all the Vrihannalas (eunuchs) trace their origin from Raja Asi.

Thereafter, entrusting the rule of Ayodhya to the best of the kings, Manu, Lord Kalki, accompanied by a large number of seers and sages, reached Mathura where he appointed the talented king Suryaketu as the king of that holy city.

While moving along this way Lord Kalki made Raja Devapi the ruler of the five kingdoms: Aristhanpur, Vrikasthala, Makanda, Hastinapur and Varanavata. Having completed all these necessary administrative assignments Lord Kalki returned to his native place Sambhal-gram (Sambhal-village). Reaching there, Lord Kalki, who loved his brothers—Kavi, Praagya, Sumantra—made them respectively the rulers of the kingdoms of Shambha, Phandra and Magadha. To his other brothers from his clan he awarded the rulership of Keekar, Bhavya, Karnataka, Aandhra, Uda, Kalinga, Anga, Banga etc. Thus establishing the right rulers all over the Aryavarta Lord Kalki made the rulers look after their people well and administer their kingdoms successfully.

While staying in Sambhal Lord Kalki entrusted the rule of Kankaka and Kapala region to Vishaakh Yoop Naresh. The descendants of Kritaverma were given the rulership of the central provinces called Chola, Barbar, Karva etc.

Having thus discharged his responsibilities, Lord Kalki offered his father very reverentially a variety of riches and affluence. His father, Vishnu Yasha, a Brahmana, was duly propitiated and so were the other dwellers of Sambhal who also received costly gifts from their ruler. Then he started enjoying his family life. It was only when every disorder was removed that Satya Yuga with all the four phases of Dharma dawned in all the three realms.

Lord Kalki, who granted his devotees every wish, almost brought heaven upon the earth by his intelligence, bravery and discretionary wisdom. Since pleasant and moral order prevailed upon the earth, even the seasons became very pleasant and as much tempting to even the gods that they started frequently visiting the earth to enjoy bliss in full measure. With the chaos removed and righteous order well established, the earth also became bountiful and its beings happy and healthy. All sort of vices, falsehood, thievery, diseases and afflictions almost vanished from the surface of the earth. The vile tendencies vanished on their own. Truth and righteous order reigned everywhere. The Brahmanas again became well versed in the Vedic knowledge and people became righteous. Yagyas began to be performed with great gusto. The Kshatriyas became brave and chivalrous to look after their subjects well. The trader class (Vaishya) became very honest. Engaged in the worship of Lord Vishnu they prospered well in their business. Even the Shoodras became very devoted to their masters. Life started moving smoothly on the earth once again.

Having recited this story Sootiji looked at the seers' faces for a second. They were all in a state of blissful peace. Then Shaunakji asked Sootaji: "O Sage! After worshipping Goddess Bhagwati Maya, where Raja Shashidhwaja had gone to? Please tell us in detail about Goddess Maya and the way to worship her. Also, please tell me whether the Goddess and Lord Vishnu are separable in any way?"

Discovering Shaunak Sage's curiosity about Goddess Maya Sootaji said: "O Sages! The same question was once put by the great Sage Markandeya before Shukadevaji. The way Shukadeva essayed to answer this question is also what I am doing with my own comprehension. Now listen to the greatness of Goddess Maya, listening whose glories fulfils all one's desires and the worldly afflictions also get cured." When Lord Vishnu's great devotee Maharaj Shashidhwaja left his huge Bhallat Nagar, he had chanted the following verse: "*Om hleenkaarmayee,*" the essence of all truth, purest divinity Mayadevi! You are the mother of all gods. Even Vedas chant your glory. All the material objects remain hidden in your womb. You are the nemesis of all those who are vile and the chosen deity of all the noble persons. I reverence thee with my total devotion.

"O Bhagwati! You are beyond all the realms, yet part of them; you are ever adored by all the learned sages like Vyasa are Vashishtha and even Lord Narayan chants verses in your praise. You are ever amove in the waves of time. Your sportive plays are so overwhelming that all the beings keep on getting entangled in them. O Bhagwati! I ever seek your shelter. You are ever present whether it be the time of Pralaya, creation or destruction. No ordained action gets ever completed without your all-encompassing grace. I reverence such an Omnipotent Goddess. You pervade every part of the universe. You are Lakshmi, Saraswati, Parvati and every female power of this universe. You are the child goddess in early age and the full-fledged goddess in your youth. In every form you are ever adorable. You are the cosmic power that keeps this whole creation live. In anger you are Goddess Chandi, in knowledge you are Savitri and in punishing the wicked you are Goddess Durga yourself. You are the veritable source of all light in the universe and hence the object of divine adoration. He upon whom you shed your grace has his all wishes fulfilled and all dreams realised. I bow to you Great Goddess!"

Telling about Raja Shashidhwaja's prayer to Goddess Mahamaya – as told by Shukadevaji to sage Markandeya – Sootaji told the assembly that as the prayer was finished, the king went to heaven (Vaikuntha) even while in the mortal body from a place called Kokamukha. This way he attained Moksha.

As Lord Kalki re-established his hold on the world, righteous order began to reign and people had grown very religious and god-fearing as they should be in the Satya Age. The spirit took precedence over the form and all sort of hypocrisy and double play ended.

Once when peace dawned all over the plenum and everything was quite in order, his mortal father, Vishnu Yasha, asked him (Lord Kalki) to perform the Yagya gratifying the gods.

Lord Kalki was glad to get this request from his father and reassured him that soon he would be performing Rajasooya and Ashwamedha Yagya and this way "I hope to gratify my fount, Lord Vishnu, as well." For this purpose he invited Kripacharya, Parashuram, Vashistha, Vyas, Dhaumya, Akrita Vrana, Ashvatthama, Madhu-Chchanda, Mandapaal and all the top seers and sages of the Age. After duly welcoming them and adoring them with the help of holy waters, he made them choose a site amidst Ganga and Yamuna for the Yagya. Then he took his ceremonial bath and fed the Brahmanas on choicest edibles of the age, to be eaten by sucking, chewing or swallowing.

In order to ensure trouble-free Yagya Lord Kalki ceremonially invited Agni . Varuna was invoked to ensure non-stop water supply, wind-god for serving the oblation evenly to all. He ensured that nothing should be found wanting for the performance of any Yagya. All the population of his realms were liberally fed. The Apsaras (divine-danseuses) also graced the occasion to provide fun to the function. The Gandharvas sang the 'hoo-hoo' songs. When the Yagya rituals were ritually gone through, with the permission of his father, Lord Kalki decided to stay for some days more on the bank of the holy river Ganga. Meanwhile, Brahmana Vishnu Yasha began to enlighten people with his sermons on the moral teaching.

While everything was in its proper order and peace reigned everywhere, there happened to reach sage Narada, playing upon his celestial lute. He was also accompanied by the Gandharva Lord, Tumburoo. Vishnu Yasha rushed at the gate to welcome the two dignitaries and expressed his great delight at getting an opportunity to welcome the two renowed Vishnu devotees: "I am sure by getting your Darshan I must not only be making my life blessed but even my manes also duly gratified." After the pleasantries were over Vishnu Yasha requested Narada to enlighten on the divine (spiritual) knowledge and the role of Maya in it.

Naradaji said: "O Great Brahamana! When the body perishes the soul still longs to get it back. The dialogue that took place between the soul (Jeeva) and Maya is being recounted by me for your benefit. Now listen to it very carefully as its listening is enough to grant the listener Moksha. Bhagwati Maya, adopting the form of a graceful lady on the mount-range of Vindhyachala, accosted the soul this way: "I am Maya! When I have abandoned you, why must you desire life back?" Jeeva (soul) replied: "O Maya! I don't want life back but basic meaning or manifestation of life is body. That is necessary for getting an identity. Although identity leads to arrogance yet one cannot get it without a body." Whereupon Maya said: "But identity leads to separation of the existences. Why must you have this realisation when you know that everything essentially has One Origin? Since without manifestation no activity is possible, how do you act in the absence of Maya (myself)?"

Clarifying its importance Jeeva said: "O Maya! Remember that you exist through me only. Separated from me you have no entity. As the rise of the sun dispels or destroys all darkness, the same way you shall perish in my absence. You look enchanting like the clouds around the sun since you derive strength from me only. While you keep the world under delusion, unless you have a conscious soul, you cannot exist. Remember that you are only the halo around the luminary – Lord Vishnu – and you exist because I see you exist. Those who know this reality are not hoodwinked by Maya and in that case the Jeeva (soul) stays ever in communion with eternity."

Having got this highly enlightening sermon from Narada ji and learning that Lord Kalki, his son, verily Lord Vishnu himself, Vishnu Yasha decided to leave for forest as he found his all objectives accomplished and dreams realised. With full rituals he discarded his family life to reach Badrikashram with his wife where soon he quitted his mortal coil. When his wife saw him going back to the Supreme Spirit, she also breathed her last. The message of his parents' death was conveyed to Lord Kalki by the peripatetic mendicants. He was quite sad but relieved to know that they met a timely death. Then with due ceremony he performed his obsequies rituals and began to devote most of his time in Sambhal Gram.

Once, after some time, Sage Parashuram happened to come down from his Mahendra Parvat on way to his performing pilgrimage. This sudden arrival of his guru delighted Lord Kalki and his wife. Very respectfully they welcomed their Guru and satisfied him in every way. Then, once in the afternoon when Parashuram got up from his siesta, Lord Kalki reached his chamber and lovingly began to knead his feet. Seeking his opportunity, Lord Kalki's said: "O Sage! My wife is willing to ask a question from you." "Send her here", the sage ordered. Ramaa, wife of Lord Kalki and daughter of Raja Shashidhwaja, delightedly went to the great sage and said: "O Lord! I am content in every way. But what rankles my heart still is the fact that I am yet to get a son. Although I am quite blessed by your grace, yet a woman's life is deemed unfruitful if she doesn't produce a male child to continue his husband's lineage. Please guide me so that my wish may also be duly fulfilled."

Sootaji told the sages assembled in Nemisharanya that hearing this request from Ramaa, the spouse of Lord Kalki, Parashuram advised her to observe Rukmini Vrata. Then he enlightened her on the method, means and fruits of this Vrata. While telling her the glory of this Vrata, he narrated her the following story:

Once the demon lord Vrishaparva's daughter Sharmishtha was having bath with her friends in a stream when they detected Lord Mahadeva and his spouse Parvati's coming there. In hurry, Devyani, the daughter of the demon-mentor Shukracharya, happened to don Sharmishtha's dress. Enraged the demon-lord's daughter said, "Hey you, daughter of a begging Brahmana! How dare you wear the dress meant for me? "In anger she bound her hands with her own dress and put her into a well closeby. Devyani was helpless. After some time Raja Nahush's son, Raja Yayati, happened to pass from that well and he heard a female cry emerging from that well. Detecting a girl lying inside the well, he made her come out of it. Whereupon he learnt who that girl was. Knowing about her parentage, Yayati requested her to marry her. Then reassuring her fully, he left for his capital and Devyani went to her father Shukracharya's hermitage. There she complained against Sharmishtha's misdemeanour with her. By that time Vrishaparva, the demon-lord, had also learned about his daughter's misbehaviour with Devyani. He came to his mentor and said: "O Gurudeva! I know that my daughter has misbehaved with Devyani. I am ready to face my punishment for her." Whereupon Devyani said: "I want Sharmishtha to serve as my maid." Thereafter, the marriage of Devyani with Raja Yayati was solemnised in which Vrishaparva gave his daughter, Sharmishtha, as the dowry-maid."

But while entrusting Sharmishtha's custody to Yayati, Shukracharya warned him that he should never summon this maid to his bed-chamber. "Else, you may become old that very moment." Yayati was so much pulverised with this warning that he made Sharmishtha stay at such a place which was beyond his sight-range. Now confined to her secluded place, Sharmishtha helplessly served her mistress, Devayani, along with other maids. Once while she was sitting depressed and wailing upon her helpless condition, she happened to spot Vishwamitra. He was surrounded by many dainty dames who were anointed with fragrant paste and they looked very charming. Many auspicious things, generally used in incense to start an auspicious ceremony, were lying before them. There Sage Vishwamitra prepared and laid a lotus flower with eight petals, flanked by four banana plants planted at the four corners of the holy altar. Under that canopy were placed many beautiful idols of Lord Vasudeva. There were many Brahmanas chanting the holy Shlokas and worshipping the idol with all the sixteen modes of worship. They were chanting the holy modes of worship. They were chanting the holy words meaning: "O Lord of Rukmini, Supreme Lord Vasudeva, please accept the oblation prepared with Durva and sandalwood. O Lord, all these offerings have been collected from all over the world. Please accept them with your eternal spouse Lakshmi...." This way when Sharmishtha saw the ladies very devoutly offering the oblations to Lord Krshna (Vasudeva) and Rukmini she also came forward and told sage Vishwamitra and other ladies present there: "Listen ye all to the succour of an unfortunate woman. Although I am a princess, my misfortune has deprived me of the conjugal bliss." Having learnt about her tale of woe Vishwamitra also made her perform the Rukmini Vrata which ensured her getting close to her husband and enjoy conjugal bliss. This vrata had also been performed by Draupadi under the influence of Vribadashwa which made her get over all her affection. So following Parashuram's instructions, Lord Kalki's wife Ramaa also observed this Vrata. At the conclusion of this endeavour, Parashuram offered her Kheer. The effect of the Vrata and its offering was her getting two sons named Meghamaal and Balahaka who were very noble, obedient, intelligent and god-fearing. Now Ramaa had all her desires fulfilled. She had Lord Kalki as her husband and two very able sons to grant her all mortal bliss. Now ;·'th the world having peace and plenty and righteous orac. very well established Lord Kalki with his spouse Ramaa and sons enjoyed his stay in his native place for about a millennium.

Narrating this story of Lord Kalki Sutaji said to the Brahmanas that he had told them the holy story with all the necessary details. "Now I tell you about the deeds that Lord Kalki accomplished during his last phase. The listener of this tale shall also enjoy all the heavenly and secular happiness and shall reap great rewards in all of his endeavours.

"During the last millennium the glory of Sambhal Gram had become incomparable in the entire universe. There were as many as sixty-eight holy places that had assembled in that native place of Lord Kalki. Owing to Kalkiji's personal influence any one who died in Sambhal Gram attained Moksha immediately. Nature and all the heavenly forces ensured the best of everything in Sambhal. Seasons were pleasant and climate was most conducive to good health.

Once while going for a ride in the chariot provided by Indra, Lord Kalki, with his wife Padma went to a far place and getting down from his chariot entered a cave laden with blue gems. He was followed by his two wives Padma and Ramaa accompanied by his scores of maids.

All of a sudden Padma espied Lord Kalki, glittering like a rain-laden blue cloud, reposing amidst very comely dames. Ramaa also reached there and she was as sad as Padma had grown when they both compared themselves with those wenches. Although both of them were getting sexually charged imagining Lord Kalki's closeness, they felt rather depressed in the imagined comparison. All of a sudden they found Kalkiji close to them. The Lord knew secret of every heart. Like the maddened she-elephants rush to the males at the peak of their heat, so did both Ramaa and Padma. They felt delighted that their fear was beseless as Lord Kalki never ditched his any devotee, male or female.

This way Lord Kalki continued to reign in Sambhal Gram and ensured that Satya Yuga-like conditions stayed in the world.

Epilogue

While narrating the Kalki Purana Sootaji told the assembled sages: "Once Lord Kalki was seated on his throne in Sambhal Gram when all the gods led by Brahma reached there for his Darshan. At that time Sambhal appeared more enchanting and beautiful than even the divinities' capital, Amaravati. His yellow garment from which his dark blue body hue glowed with an enchanting radiance looked captivating. The crown emitting soft glow and a typical fragrance was reposed on his head. The crocodile-formed ear rings gave the impression as though two moons were shining close to his face – the sun. The gods collectively hymned him with great fervour: "O Great Lord! Master of the universe, repository of all that is good, auspicious and beautiful, the mere glance of whom ensures all welfare to the beholder, O Omnipotent, Indomitable, the very fount of all energies, we offer our prayers and seek your gratification. O Lord! As this earth has the rule of propriety, righteousness and morality very well established, we request you to grace your permanent abode in Vaikunth and leave this mortal plane."

Hearing these reverential words Lord Kalki was extremely happy and he also decided that it was about time he went back to Vaikuntha. Immediately he consulted his priest and had the precious time appointed for making his all the four sons well established upon the throne. Then he invited his people of Shambhal and disclosed that he was willing to leave the earth on the divinities' request.

The people felt as though this was a bolt from the blue. They couldn't even imagine staying in Samhbal without the active protection provided by Lord Kalki. They all requested him not to leave them in lurch and in case his decision was final then he should also take all the people along. "We don't want to stay in this transistory world in your absence. Although the worldly attraction do bind us, we can't imagine staying here in your absence."

Lord Kalki gave them a sermon then, full of the knowledge of the essence, explaining that each entity had its purpose of stay in the world and no one could stay here purposelessly. At last the people agreed but some of them still followed him to the jungle to where Lord Kalki, forsaking all worldly possessions, left with his two wives. Taking the holy bath in the river Ganga he reached a cave in the Himalayas and sat their in his four-armed form. Each of his four poor arms had one object. One of them had the Shankh (conch-shell), the other Chakra (discus), the third a mace and the fourth one a lotus. Immediately he was surrounded by the high seers and the gods who began to hymn him in a devout unison. As he entered his eternal Vishnu form, the ensuing light from the transition radiated the entire plenum and his Darshan of the Eternal Form became available for every being.

In compliance with Lord Kalki's instruction Dharma and Satya (Yuga) accepted to remain firm on the earth. Raja Manu and Devapi accepted to help Lord Kalki's sons to look after general administration of the law and order. As the news of Lord Kalki's departure to his eternal abode reached Raja Vishaakh Yoop, he also quitted his mortal coil through observance of a strict penance. In fact most of the kings did the same. But owing to Lord Kalki's grace this transition was swift and smooth and no disturbance occurred anywhere in the world.

Having heard Lord Kalki's tale Shukadeva also repaired to Nar-Narayana hermitage in Badrikashram. High sages like Markandeya and others also left for their respective hermitages.

The hearing of this Purana-Katha ensures freedom from all the affliction of this Kali Yuga and the listener never deviates from the righteous path. Due to the curiosity expressed by sage Shaunak, the scion of Bhrigu's family, all the sages could listen from Sootaji this highly enlightening and affliction-destroying tale of Lord Kalki's incarnation on the Earth to redeem it from the vices and wickedness let loose during this phase by Kali Age. However, some sages still wanted to know that when Lord Kalki repaired to his eternal abode, how did he worship the great river Ganga. Sootaji told the 'Ganga Stavan' (Prayer for Ganga) which was recited by Lord Kalki and other sages in Haridwar. "O divine river Ganga! You, having issued from the feet of Lord Vishnu, are now taking across the beings of this mortal world. You destroy all the sins of this vile age. Following the path suggested by Raja Bhagirath, on your way you had browbeaten the vehicle of Indra, Eiravat, and were lost in the tendril locks of Lord Shiv. You are as sin-redeeming as Lord Shankar's grace as you tangibly represent the same. Your origin is water-pot of Lord Brahma. (When in the process of measuring all the three realms with his three steps, Lord Vishnu, as Vaman, placed his foot on the heavenly plane, Brahma washed it very reverentially. It is that water which has emerged as the river of Ganga). You are dear to all as you ensure welfare of the devout. You are not only beloved of Brahma, Vishnu, Mahesh but of every being who is god-fearing and noble. You were also the wife of Shantanu and mother of Devvrata, renowned as Bhishma due to his terrible vow. O Tripaksha Devi! Bless us that our body gets your touch every day and even after death you will rid it of all the afflictions. O Bhagwati Ganga, O Mateshwari, I bow to you."

Narrating the 'Stavan' Sootaji said that he had heard about this prayer from Shri Shukadevaji. Reading and listening this prayer enhances the aspirant's age and keeps him beyond the reach of the Kali afflictions.

The Kalki Purana, like any other Purana, ends with summarising all its events, happening in a chronological order. Those who read this Purana with concentrated devotion stay away from all the Kali-induced woes. If a Brahmana reads or listens it, he gets all the knowledge and stays content; the Kshatriya all valour and kingly ruches; the Vaishya all commercial success and wealth and the Shoodra all sorts of physical comforts. Those desirous of wealth get wealth; of knowledge knowledge; of discretion discretion. In short this Purana's reading or listening fills the listener or reader with a supreme delight which Vedavyas must have felt when he composed it.

The Kalki Purana again asserts the well-established fact that Lord Vishnu is Supreme as he is the only one among the Triumvirate who has the power to incarnate his image on the earth to rid it from all troubles. Victory to Lord Vishnu whose incarnation is Lord Kalki!

BOOKS FOR ALL

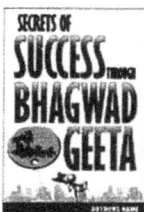

DIAMOND BOOKS X-30, Okhla Industrial Area, Phase-II New Delhi-110020
Tel : 91+11-40712100, 40716600 email : sales@dpb.in www.dpb.in

www.ingramcontent.com/pod-product-compliance
Lightning Source LLC
Chambersburg PA
CBHW051848040426